Magna Carta

The True Story Behind the Charter

David Starkey

HODDER

First published in Great Britain in 2015 by Hodder & Stoughton
An Hachette UK company

First published in paperback in 2016

1

A CIP catalogue record for this title is available from the British Library

ISBN 978 1 473 61007 1

Typeset in Fournier MT by Palimpsest Book Production Ltd, Falkirk, Stirlingshire

Printed and bound by CPI Group (UK) Ltd, Croydon, CR0 4YY

Hodder & Stoughton policy is to use papers that are natural,
renewable and recyclable products and made from wood grown in
sustainable forests. The logging and manufacturing processes are expected
to conform to the environmental regulations of the country of origin.

Hodder & Stoughton Ltd
Carmelite House
50 Victoria Embankment
London EC4Y 0DZ

www.hodder.co.uk

In piam memoriam

G. R. E

CONTENTS

INTRODUCTION

J ust over a hundred years ago the preparations for the 700th anniversary of Magna Carta were well underway. The lead was taken by the Royal Historical Society. With a confidence which belied the fact that the Society was itself less than forty years old, it determined that the celebrations 'should be directed by competent persons'. An international committee of the great and good was set up, with the historian and Liberal politician, Viscount Bryce, in the chair and the Archbishop of Canterbury and the Lord Mayor of London prominent among its members as representing 'the continuity of English life from 1215–1915'. 'A visit to Runnymede and an address upon the spot were contemplated' and learned essays commissioned.

Then, with only ten months to go to the anniversary, Great Britain entered the First World War on 4 August 1914 and everything was abandoned as:

> the memory of the assertion of the principle of govern-
> ment by law was overclouded by the cares of the
> immense struggle to maintain that principle through
> force of arms.

No such catastrophe has intervened to mar the celebrations of the 800th anniversary. Indeed, as I write this in the early weeks of 2015, it is clear that they will be on a scale that makes the projected events of 1915 look very small beer. They began a year early, when the prime minister held a 'one year to go' party at Downing Street on the 799th anniversary. In the year itself the British Library is mounting its largest ever exhibition. All four surviving copies of the 1215 Charter are being reunited, first in the British Library and then in the neo-gothic splendours of the Royal Gallery in the Palace of Westminster. The Declaration of Independence and the Bill of Rights are being brought over from Washington to pay tribute to their ancestral Charter here. The Queen will step into John's shoes at Runnymede on 15 June. There are displays and debates and pageants and re-enactments in The Temple and Lincoln and Salisbury and anywhere that can claim a connexion. There is a whole season of programmes on the BBC called *Taking Liberties*, of which I am presenting one. And there are books – like this.

My television programme, rather presumptuously entitled (not by me) *David Starkey's Magna Carta*, looks at the Charter in an eight-hundred-year sweep, from the thirteenth century to the present day. This book draws on the work that I did for the television programme. But its scope and intention are different. Instead of a bird's-eye view of eight centuries, it focuses on the ten years 1215 to 1225. This was the decade in which the Charter transmuted from an extremist tract into the bedrock of an evolving English constitution. The case for this view of Magna Carta is argued in detail in the text of the book; it is also presented in tabular form in the Appendix: The Charters, which prints the three crucial versions of the Charter – 1215, 1216 and 1225 – in parallel columns, and numbers and matches the chapters (or clauses).

This enables the reader to see at a glance both what stayed the same and what changed across the decade. The conclusion is inescapable: the Charter that is known to history is a product, not of the revolution coup of 1215, but of the conservative fight-back of 1216 and the consciously centrist compromise and bargain of 1225.

The story, with its remarkable cast of characters, its turbulent events and sudden reversals of fortune – not least of the Charter itself – is a fascinating one. It is also unusually well documented. Indeed, it is perhaps the first event in English history in which we can see the political process fully at work.

And that is how I try to tell it, as it happened day by day rather than with an eye to the future. Told like this, it is an antidote to some of the triumphalism of the anniversary celebrations. But my aim is not to debunk but to see if the real story of Magna Carta offers some help and guidance in our present discontents.

For, though you would not know it from the official celebrations, all is not well with the legacy of Magna Carta.

There is no overt external military threat, as in 1915. But now in 2015 there are deeper and more insidious problems. Our constitution is indeed 800 years old. And that it is is a fine and remarkable thing. But it is also showing its age and creaking at the joints. Some would even say it is suffering from terminal osteoporosis. Is it time to give up and start again? Or does looking back at where it all began in Magna Carta offer a better way?

Read and see.

The Red House
Kent
February 2015

ONE

THE GREAT KING?
JOHN AND HIS OPPONENTS

Seal of Philip Augustus

In 1212, John, King of England, Lord of Ireland and Duke of Aquitaine, seemed about to match, if not to exceed, the deeds of his greatest ancestors. There was 'no one in Ireland, Scotland and Wales', an unusually well-informed contemporary wrote, 'who did not obey his nod – something which, as is well-known, none of his predecessors had achieved'.

It was an astonishing turnaround.

John, born in 1167, was the runt of a litter of eight children: five sons and three daughters. From his father Henry II, he stood to inherit England, Normandy, Anjou, Maine and Touraine and from his mother Eleanor, Aquitaine. The resulting block of territories, known to historians as the Angevin Empire, stretched from Scotland to the Pyrenees; was the largest landmass in Europe subject to a single ruler, and dwarfed the kingdom of France, its nominal overlord.

John, nicknamed 'Lackland' as the portionless youngest son, had been prepared to do anything to get his hands on this inheritance. He had betrayed his father on his deathbed and his brother Richard in his hour of greatest need. He became king in 1199 in a disputed succession and murdered, some said with his own hand, his nephew and rival for the throne, Arthur of Brittany.

But, having waded to the throne in blood and betrayal, John then proceeded to lose, in little more than five years, the better part of his Continental inheritance. First to go was his ancestral land of Anjou, where his family were buried in the Abbey of Fontevrault under magnificently sculpted and painted effigies. Maine, Touraine and Normandy itself followed until only Aquitaine and its bordering territories were left.

John's nemesis in all this was Philip II, King of France, who had made the destruction and conquest of the Angevin Empire his life's work. Philip's life was a mirror-image of John's. He was born in 1165, the long-awaited son of the elderly Louis VII who hitherto had only daughters. Philip was crowned at fourteen; married at fifteen and became sole king on the death of his now paralysed and senile father in 1180. As king, he showed the same ruthless appetite for power as John: he persecuted and expelled the Jews; clashed with the pope; greatly expanded the royal revenues and administration, and was greedy, grasping and cunning in all his dealings.

The difference was that it worked. Partly it was luck. But Philip, much the superior politician, was also better at being bad than John. The result was that, while John's realm shrank, Philip's grew. And grew. His first biographer, the physician-turned-monk Rigord, made the fact the dominant theme of his *Life* when he surnamed Philip 'Augustus'.

'Writers', Rigord explained in his preface, 'ordinarily give the name "Augustus" (from the verb *augeo* "to make to grow or to increase") to Emperors who have *augmented* the State. Philip thus deserves the title of *Augustus* because he too has augmented the State' by so greatly increasing its territories and revenues. 'He was even', Rigord adds, 'born in *August*, the month dedicated to [the first emperor] *Augustus*, which is also the time when the barns and wine presses overflow with all the fruits of the earth.'

The contrast between this picture of plenitude and fecundity and John's nickname of 'Lackland' is dramatically perfect. But there was more to it than that. The struggle between Lackland and Augustus had also taken on the aspect of a duel: man to man. And the better man had won. All too often John had backed down or backed off or actually run away. The result was that the charge of personal cowardice was added to his other vices and he was given another, still more infamous, nickname: 'Softsword'.

It would have been hard to recover from all that. But recover John did. And quickly. Ever since the Norman Conquest English kings had been largely absentee. The loss of most of John's French lands perforce changed that and, following a truce with Philip Augustus in 1206, John concentrated on England and on raising and hoarding cash. He targeted everybody – nobles and townsmen, Jews and the Church – and he used any and every means. He was astonishingly successful. He doubled royal revenues and more, and by 1212 had accumulated a vast cash-hoard of at least £132,000, which he held in coin in a handful of castle treasuries.

One of the principal sources of John's wealth was his highly aggressive policy towards the Church. English kings – including the notably pious and papalist William the Conqueror – were determined to maintain their traditional authority over the English church. John was no exception. But he found himself confronting a formidable opponent in Innocent III. Innocent was more or less of an age with John: he became pope in 1198, a year before John's accession, and he took as high a view of his office as John did of his. Higher, even, since he claimed, in quoting the words of the prophet Jeremiah, to be 'set over the nations and over the kingdoms, to root out and to destroy, to build and to plant'.

A clash was inevitable. It came over the succession to the archbishopric of Canterbury, the primatial see of the English church. John wanted the position for the then Bishop of Norwich; Innocent determined instead to appoint Stephen Langton. The former was a typical clerical administrator and a king's man through and through; the latter was the most intellectually distinguished Englishman of his day. John, who was not without intellectual interests himself, could have stomached that. But what counted against Langton and made him wholly unacceptable to the king was that his entire academic career as both student and teacher had been spent in Paris. Paris was the beloved capital of John's great enemy, Philip Augustus. Philip walled it; paved it and lavished patronage on its schools. Langton's brother Simon, also a scholar there, was in Philip's pay, while Langton himself stood high enough in the French king's favour to have been given a prebend at Notre Dame, which provided him with a house as well as an income.

Innocent had known Langton since his own student days in Paris in the 1180s. In 1206 he summoned him to Rome and made him cardinal; the following year he persuaded a delegation of the monks of Christ Church, Canterbury to elect him archbishop. John objected vigorously. Innocent replied by praising Langton's qualities as a 'Doctor, not only in the liberal arts but also in theological learning' and then warned the king bluntly that it would be dangerous to 'fight against God and the Church in this cause for which St Thomas [Becket], that glorious martyr and archbishop, recently shed his blood'.

Innocent clearly expected John to back down. Instead the king dug in his heels and the dispute swiftly escalated into a full-scale confrontation between church and state. Both sides played tit for tat. John confiscated more and more church property; Innocent retaliated by imposing increasingly severe ecclesiastical penalties: first laying an Interdict on England in 1208; then excommunicating John in person in 1209. The spiritual loss to king and country was incalculable; but the financial benefit to John was all too easy to reckon. And John, like not a few other contemporary rulers, decided that he was happy to balance the knowable gains to his purse against the putative risks to his immortal soul.

For John's gains from the Interdict were indeed huge. The best contemporary estimate put them at £60,000, which was equivalent to two years' gross annual revenue. With wealth beyond the dreams of previous kings and an apparently iron grasp on both church and state in England, John turned outwards once more. But not to France but to Britain, where he began a showily aggressive policy towards the whole of the Celtic fringe. He imposed brutal discipline on the Anglo-Irish barons; he carried the Anglo-Norman conquest into the heart of north Wales and he disposed of the succession to the kingdom of Scotland as unchallenged overlord.

The intention was clear: John would replace his father's lost Angevin Empire with a new, more durable dominion over the British Isles.

But, at the moment the vision seemed about to turn into reality, everything fell to pieces.

TWO

THE CRISIS

Battle of Bouvines

In August 1212 John was at Nottingham to oversee another punitive expedition against the Welsh. It was intended to shock and awe: there was a mass hanging of twenty-eight Welsh hostages and the naval and military might of England was ordered to muster at Chester.

But treason struck first. On 16 August, only two days after the mass hanging, John learned of a major baronial plot against his life and throne. He was to be murdered or abandoned to the Welsh, and Simon de Montfort, the leader of the Albigensian Crusade, chosen as king in his place.

Shaken, the king abandoned the Welsh expedition. Hostages were demanded from those he suspected of involvement and two important barons, Robert Fitzwalter and Eustace de Vescy, fled with their families and households to France and the ever-welcoming arms of Philip Augustus.

From this moment, the Barnwell chronicler wrote, John suspected everyone and he would go nowhere without an armed bodyguard. More importantly, his confidence faltered and he threw his aggressive policies into reverse.

It was a transparent bid for support. Instead, his apparent strength collapsed like a house of cards.

*

Fitzwalter and de Vescy both had personal quarrels with John. Fitzwalter also had the reputation of being quarrelsome, impetuous and swift to resort to violence in support of his claims. But, petty though their individual motives may have been, the two men represented forces bigger than themselves. De Vescy was an important landowner in the north while Fitzwalter was lord of Dunmow in Essex and Baynard's Castle in London. London and the north were both to be major centres of opposition to John. As indeed – and famously – was the baronial class as a whole.

The barons, with their rich lands on both sides of the Channel, had been the great beneficiaries of the Conquest. They were correspondingly badly affected by John's loss of his French territories. They were also, as the king's direct dependants and a sort of extended family, the group that experienced most immediately John's elevation of caprice into a principle of policy.

Even in matters of justice. The half-century before John's accession had seen an enormous expansion in law and administration with his father, Henry II, playing the key role. Henry was a skilled lawyer himself. He was, according to our greatest legal historian, 'quite competent to criticize minutely the wording of a charter; to frame a new clause and to give his vice-chancellor lessons in conveyancing'.

But Henry II's greatest achievement was to impose his justice even in his absence. This he did through the development of the writ or standardised royal letter. The writ was written out on a slip of parchment and authenticated by attaching the great seal. In the course of Henry II's reign, writs were developed to deal with all the most common legal problems of the king's subjects. They were mass produced and they were available, for a fee, to every freeman. Previously the king's justice had depended on the king's actual presence; now, with the writ, the seal and the magic of writing, the king and his justice could be everywhere, for everybody.

For most of the king's subjects, the gains were immense and John, in this regard at least, was eager to follow in his father's footsteps. He was his equal in his interest in administration and knowledge of its most arcane details; his tutor had been a leading judge and he found the judicial role a congenial one. He even began his reign by issuing a grandiloquently worded, 'Constitution', which reformed – and, it claimed, reduced – the charges for issuing the great seal.

But law and justice are a two-edged sword. They are a vital necessity. On the other hand, with the king frequently intervening in the judicial process and acting as judge himself, justice could easily be perverted. It could become excessive, arbitrary and a mere cloak for money grubbing. And the richer the litigant, the greater the temptation.

Once again, the loss of John's French territories seems to mark a turning point. Ambitious barons, like kings themselves, sought to increase their power by pursuing dynastic policies: they wanted to transmit their lands and titles to their heirs; marry well themselves and obtain rich wards for their offspring to marry in turn. Each one of these processes required the king's agreement and it was sold at a price. And, in the cases of the richest estates, wardships and marriages, at a very high price indeed.

All of which was acceptable and well understood. But it was also well understood that the king would not be too rigorous in pursuing the theoretically ruinous debts that were the price of baronial ambition. After 1207 John broke this convention, as he broke so many others. That year, the lands of the Earl of Leicester were declared forfeit for the non-payment of debt. Even more sensationally, in 1208 John turned against his erstwhile favourite, William de Briouze. The de Briouze estates were seized; William and his family driven into exile, and his wife and eldest son imprisoned at Windsor Castle where, it was generally believed, they were starved to death in hideous circumstances.

John's own explanation for this atrocity was that he was invoking the penalties for the non-payment of debt 'in accordance with the custom of our kingdom and the law of the Exchequer'.

With John on the throne, the law, it seemed, meant just what the king chose it to mean, neither more nor less. The barons, for their part, drew their own conclusion.

Once they were safely in France, Fitzwalter and de Vescy found a wide and sympathetic audience for their grievances

– including the king, the papal legate and their fellow exiles from England. They seem to have tailored their story to suit. They told Philip Augustus that John had assaulted the honour of their womenfolk (his daughter, in the case of Fitzwalter; his wife, in the case of de Vescy). To the papal legate, Pandulf, they span a more improving tale and solemnly explained that they had rebelled because of their outrage at the Interdict and their conscientious refusal to serve an excommunicated king. What they said to their fellow English exiles, who included William de Briouze's son Giles, Bishop of Hereford, and Stephen Langton, the papal candidate as Archbishop of Canterbury, is unknown. But it was enough to establish a clear community of interest, and they swiftly became allies, perhaps even friends.

Hitherto, the two principal foci of opposition to John – the baronial and the ecclesiastical – had been separate and distinct. Now, in Paris, in the fevered world of exile and with Philip Augustus as the eager go-between, they fused and became one.

It would be hard to exaggerate the consequences.

John took steps to regain the political initiative. He sought to unite his friends – or at least those who were not inveterately opposed to him – by launching another attack on the old enemy, Philip Augustus of France. At the same time, he tried to divide his enemies by agreeing terms with the pope. The two schemes came together on 15 May 1213 at

Ewell near Dover. There John knelt and made a formal surrender of his kingdom to the papal legate Pandulf in the presence of the large army he had assembled to resist Philip Augustus's threatened counter-invasion of England.

But all turned to dust and ashes. John's schemes against France crashed to absolute defeat, with Philip's rout of the allied English, Flemish and Imperial armies at the battle of Bouvines on 27 July 1214. Still worse, the terms of John reconciliation with Innocent III included the return and restoration of his leading baronial opponents, Fitzwalter and de Vescy. And, worst of all, the campaign of 1214 exhausted his cash-hoard.

Impoverished, at bay at home and abroad, John lay naked to his enemies. They had no reason to spare him.

THREE

REBELS WITH A CAUSE

The enthronement of a bishop

On 13 October 1214 John returned from his ill-fated French expedition. He landed at Dartmouth to find that England, which he had milked so long, had become ungovernable. The challenge to royal power began with a general taxpayers' strike. Then opposition started to coalesce and take shape and structure. Its leaders – with the returned exiles Robert Fitzwalter and Eustace de Vescy to the fore – were the usual baronial suspects. But their tactics were new. Radically so.

Revolts against royal misgovernment – and there had been many – typically took the form of rebellion in favour of a rival claimant to the throne. That had been tried in the abortive baronial plot of 1212. But de Montfort had not been a compelling candidate and there was no one much better on the horizon two or three years later. John's murder of Arthur had eliminated his obvious legitimate rival and his own children were too young. This meant John's opponents risked being rebels without a cause.

They escaped the dilemma by taking the revolutionary step of rebelling in the name, not of a *person*, but of an *idea*: a detailed programme of legal and governmental reform to be embodied in the form of a solemn act or charter. Their campaign ended – famously – in John's granting of the Great Charter at Runnymede.

How and when it began is much less clear.

There was, of course, one new man in English politics who was destined to play a central – though much debated – part in the lead-up to Magna Carta: Stephen Langton. Langton's role was difficult, not least because he was the servant of two – or even three – masters: the king, to whom he swore fealty after his long-delayed admission as archbishop; the baronial opposition, with whom his contacts went back to at least 1211, when he had officiated at the funeral of the exiled ex-favourite, William de Briouze at the Abbey of St Victor in Paris; and, above all, the pope.

Innocent set out Langton's position in his instructions of 15 July 1213. He was to 'do all that you believe to be helpful to the salvation and peace of the king and kingdom, not forgetting the honour and advantage of the Apostolic See and the English church'. The balancing act required was complex and it quickly became impossible, not least because of Innocent's own volcanic interventions. Langton probably recognised this. Nevertheless he set himself to discharge his Sisyphean task with his accustomed conscientiousness.

Langton returned to England on 9 July 1213 and on the 20th at Winchester he presided at a solemn ceremony of reconciliation. The archbishop absolved the king from his excommunication and celebrated mass in his presence; the king in turn swore an oath. Quite what, is not known. Nor is it clear whether John took the oath of his own volition or whether he was impelled by Langton. But the best guess is that, readmitted to the congregation of the faithful, the king responded by renewing his coronation oath with its threefold promise: to preserve peace and protect the Church; to maintain good laws and abolish bad, and to dispense justice to all.

That was momentous enough. But John's opponents and monastic chroniclers alike were quick to inflate the event still further and invest it with an overtly 'constitutional' significance. They made John's absolution conditional upon his taking the oath. They claimed that the oath had included a promise to preserve the ancient baronial liberties which had been confirmed by the charters of his predecessors. And they named Langton as the man who brought the most important of these charters – the coronation charter of Henry I – to the attention of contemporaries and made them aware of its significance.

Roger of Wendover, the most circumstantial of these writers, even named the day when and the place where the revelation took place: 25 August 1214 at St Paul's Cathedral in London. 'At this conference', Wendover states, Langton 'called some of the nobles aside to him'; reminded them of John's oath at Winchester and informed them that 'a charter of Henry I . . . has just now been found, by which you may, if you wish it, recall your long-lost rights and your former condition'.

He then exhibited the document to general view and ordered the charter to be read out aloud so that everybody could hear it.

It is a good story. But it is told only by Wendover. And even he records it as no more than rumour: '*as report asserts*'. Nor is the rumour borne out by the facts. Langton was certainly at St Paul's on that day and we have the text of the sermon he preached. But nowhere does he make any mention of the charter of Henry I or anything like it; instead his concerns were purely and properly pastoral.

This surely is the point. Wendover's story is fundamentally implausible because it presents Langton in a false light, as the theoretician and leader of the baronial cause. In short, as a partisan. Now Langton could be – and was – vigorously partisan where the interests of the Church were involved. But in matters of state his role – as required both by Innocent's instructions and the dictates of his own conscience – was go-between and peacemaker.

His life would have been much easier had it been otherwise.

Nevertheless, with or (much more likely) without Langton's advocacy, the charter of Henry I took centre stage in the autumn of 1214. The rout of Bouvines had opened the floodgates of opposition to John. The clamour for a renewal of Henry I's charter concentrated the flow and turned it into an irresistible mill-race.

The charter was a well-known and widely distributed document. There were copies in several archives, including those of the exchequer, the city of London and the see of Canterbury. Wendover even found a copy, addressed to 'all (Henry's) faithful subjects, as well French as English, in Hertfordshire', in his own backyard at St Alban's and transcribed it into his chronicle. It had been confirmed by Henry II. And it is easy to see what made it so attractive to John's baronial opponents.

Two things stand out. The first, on which most attention has focused, is the charter's high-minded denunciation of recent corruption on the one hand, and its invocation of good old times on the other, with its references to 'the law of King Edward (the Confessor)' or to the practice 'in King Edward's time'. Actually, the references are rather few (only three in a substantial document). And the prose in which they are expressed is distinctly penny-plain.

Much more grandiloquent, and characteristically tuppence-coloured, is John's own inaugural 'Constitution'. John attributed his accession to a threefold title: 'hereditary right', 'divine mercy or providence' and 'the consent and favour of a unanimous clergy and people'. He proclaimed that 'his supreme wish and duty' was to provide for 'the liberty and safety of clergy and people'; 'to abolish evil and inequitable customs, whether they had arisen from cupidity, lack of good counsel or any other depravity of mind'; and to do everything 'for the honour of God and Holy Church and the peace and tranquillity of clergy and people'.

In short, if the barons had wanted in fine words, John's inaugural 'Constitution' supplied them in abundance. But they showed no interest in it. Why, I wonder? Manifestly because they did not trust John. But also, I think, because they did not much trust fine words either.

This is where Henry I's charter really comes in. It may have been relatively short on fine words. But it was long on detailed provisions about inheritance, wardship and marriage that were the key issues in dispute between John and his barons. And this, I would argue, is why it was so attractive to John's rebellious baronage in the winter of 1214–15. It was not a question of vague appeals to a righteous past or still less of sonorous phrases about a better future. The barons were not Wilsonian idealists or monastic chroniclers or schoolmen like Langton or modern constitutional theorists, who all one way or another tend to be professionally in thrall to the magic of language. They were practical men who wanted practical solutions to practical problems. And they realised that Henry I's charter offered just that. Some of its provisions applied directly to their present predicament; others needed only lightly reworking; while the whole provided a model in miniature for a comprehensive reconstruction of law and government.

The road to Runnymede was to be walked by men with their feet firmly on the ground, not with their heads in the clouds. And it was the charter of Henry I that pointed the way.

FOUR

THE ROAD TO RUNNYMEDE

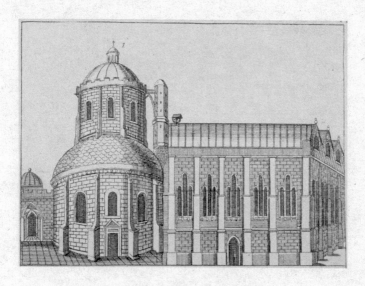

Temple Church, London

The royal Christmas festivities marked only the briefest lull in this winter of discontent. John spent the feast itself at Winchester – limiting the celebrations to a single day, according to Wendover – before hastening back to London to confront his rebellious vassals. They met on 6 January 1215. This was the last of the twelve days of Christmas and the feast of the Epiphany or Three Kings, when kings wore the crown and kingship itself was celebrated.

This year, instead, John's crown tottered. His subjects came armed and determined. John, impoverished and hopelessly weakened politically, had lost the initiative. And, despite his tenacity and cunning, he would never fully regain it. In England. Abroad it was a different matter as his surrender of his kingdom to Innocent III had procured him a powerful if unexpected ally.

There were only two problems. The first was distance. The swiftest messenger took at least sixty days to ride to and from Rome. This meant that Innocent's interventions in English politics, while always forceful, were often hopelessly out of step with events. The second was more fundamental. Back in the days of the Interdict, John had treated papal fulminations with indifference if not contempt. As a newly minted papal vassal, he had changed his tune. But his barons remained as coolly unmoved as ever. They paid lip-service to Rome and they sued for Innocent's approval. But when they failed to get it they carried on regardless.

And there was nothing that Innocent – or John – could do.

The meeting on 6 January took place in the New Temple in London. Built in the latest fashionable – and very French – gothic style and modelled on the circular church of the Holy Sepulchre in Jerusalem, the church and its huge precinct were the headquarters in England of the immensely rich, immensely powerful, crusading order of the Knights Templar. On the western border of the City of London but not part of it, the Temple was a sort of neutral, privileged territory in which both John and his opponents could feel safe.

At the meeting, the gap between the two sides proved unbridgeable. The barons, who arrived armed, demanded John agree to confirm the charter of Henry I. John, on grounds of the unheard-of novelty of their demands, pleaded for delay.

Both sides now took unprecedented steps. The barons, tacitly supported by some of the bishops, seem to have entered into a formal *conjuratio*, or sworn undertaking, to obtain the confirmation of the charter come what may:

pledging themselves 'to sustain the house of the Lord and stand fast for the liberty of the church and the realm'. John countered with an oath of his own and demanded the barons swear the traditional oath of allegiance but with an added clause: to hold with him not only against all men *but also against the charter*.

After the January meeting had ended in deadlock, John sought to buy time. He granted the barons a safe conduct to Low Sunday (26 April), which marked the end of the Easter celebrations. He also promised to meet them on that day at Northampton and give them an answer. Both king and barons used the interval to manoeuvre for advantage. There were two campaigns. The first, to gain papal endorsement, saw a runaway victory by John. He cemented his triumph by 'taking the cross' on 4 March: that is, he took the vows of a crusader. Already a papal vassal, he was now as a crusader absolutely under the protection of the Church.

John's position was confirmed by three letters despatched from Rome on 19 March. They differed markedly in tone. In the first, Innocent gently enjoined John to hear the just petitions of his barons and treat them kindly. In the second, addressed to the barons, the pope brusquely condemned their leagues and conspiracies to press claims on the king by force of arms; ordered them to abandon any such on pain of excommunication; and required them to make requests of the king, not with insolence, but with due reverence for his royal honour. While in the third letter, Langton received the sharpest rebuke of all: not only had he failed as a mediator, Innocent declared, he had even been an occasion of dispute since the baronial claims had only arisen after his return to England. He was to make amends forthwith by bringing the two sides to agreement.

As far as Innocent was concerned, this *triplex forma pacis* ('triple form of peace') settled the rights and wrongs of the matter in a fashion that was 'honest, reasonable and acceptable to all God-fearing men'. Thus spoke Rome. But here, where it counted, men, God-fearing and otherwise, begged to differ. For another campaign was being waged, with a very different outcome. This was a battle for hearts and minds in England. It soon turned into a real war, if a brief and limited one. And, after a shaky start, it was won hands down by the barons.

Easter, and the date of the projected meeting at Northampton between the king and barons, was now approaching. The two sides, as ever, reacted very differently. The barons were confident and organised; the king defensive, dilatory and evasive. As Easter week began (that is, around 13 April) the northern barons assembled under arms at Stamford and marched south. They were joined en route by Robert Fitzwalter and Geoffrey Mandeville from East Anglia and, by the time they reached the vicinity of Northampton, they had become a substantial force.

John meanwhile had decided to break his word yet again. He would not come to Northampton; instead on 23 April he issued a safe conduct, which ran till 28 May, to all who would come to speak with him through the mediation of Archbishop Langton.

The baronial forces now continued their march south, overshooting Northampton and bivouacking at Brackley, a manor owned by Saer de Quincy, Earl of Winchester and sworn brother-in-arms of Robert Fitzwalter. There the barons turned from arms to words and drew up a list of their demands. When Langton and the other royal emissaries turned up, they were given the schedule and a blunt ultimatum:

Unless the king immediately granted (their demands) and confirmed them under his own seal, they would, by taking possession of his fortresses, force him to give them sufficient satisfaction as to their before-named demands.

It was a direct threat of civil war.

Langton and his fellows returned to the king 'and read to him the heads of the (schedule) one by one'. John denounced the barons' demands 'as vain and visionary and . . . unsupported by any plea of reason' and swore 'that he would never grant them such liberties as would render him their slave'.

Their ultimatum rejected, the barons carried out their threat. On 5 May, they renounced their fealty or allegiance. They appointed Robert Fitzwalter their commander-in-chief, and – in a clear riposte to John's taking of the cross – gave him the title of 'marshal of the army of God and Holy Church'. Then they marched off to lay siege to John's castle of Northampton.

Here they met their first reverse. They had come without siege engines and they suffered their first fatalities, including Fitzwalter's standard-bearer. 'In confusion', they lifted their siege and marched to Bedford.

John countered with two initiatives, one peaceable, the other warlike. At the beginning of May he made his first formal concessions to the rebels: on the 9th he referred 'all the issues and articles which (the barons) seek of us' to a commission, consisting of the pope as chairman and eight barons, four royalist and four rebel; and on the 10th he declared that 'he would not arrest or disseise (the rebel barons) or their men nor would he go against them by force of arms except by the law of the land and by judgment of their peers in his court'. Then, after the carrot, there came the stick, as, two days later on 12 June, John ordered the seizure of the estates of the rebels.

It was now the rebels' move in this so-far rather careful game of point counter-point. By his charter of 9 May, John had set up a commission of arbitration. Commissions need submissions. And the barons, with their impressive tactical dexterity, produced one to order. It was, I would suggest, the so-called 'unknown charter'.

This document, which has puzzled historians since its discovery over a century ago, consists of a copy of the coronation charter of Henry I, followed by a list of twelve actual or proposed concessions by John. The two parts of the document are linked with an explanatory heading: 'This is the charter of King Henry by which the barons seek their liberties; and this *consequentia* King John concedes.' The first of the ensuing concessions takes the form of a third-person statement: 'King John concedes that he will not take a man without judgment, nor accept anything for doing justice, nor do injustice'; the remaining eleven are all couched, most unroyally, in the first person singular ('I concede, I grant, I ought').

The key word of course is *consequentia*. *Consequentia* is a technical term, but of logic not of law. It means a 'chain of reasoning or argument'. In other words, the concessions which John makes are seen as the logical corollary of his acknowledgment of the charter of Henry I as an authoritative statement of liberties. There is also the implication that the individual concessions follow on from each other.

The 'unknown charter' was thus the perfect riposte to John's initiatives of 9 and 10 May. Its quasi-academic tone, established by the use of the term *consequentia*, was nicely calculated for a document which was to be placed before a panel of arbitrators presided over by a former scholar of

Paris like Innocent III. It took, or affected to take, seriously the king's willingness to submit to the panel 'all the issues and articles which (the barons) seek of us' and pointed out the logical consequences. It also took on board the king's fine words about justice in the letters patent of 10 May but, rather less respectfully, suggested that they would be meaningful only if they were tied down to specifics as *per* the ensuing list of eleven further concessions.

And so things stood in the middle of May. Rome had fulminated; John had prevaricated and the barons had demonstrated. In the circumstances, the 'unknown charter' offered much the most likely way out of the crisis. The charter of Henry I, whose confirmation had been called for since the previous winter of discontent, would have been reissued. There would have been additional reinforcing clauses, with the king's promises on justice being given pride of place. And it would, almost certainly, have been the merest footnote in history.

But then everything was changed by the events of a single day. Robert Fitzwalter, the rebel commander and 'marshal of the army of God and Holy Church' was, as lord of Dunmow, a great landowner in East Anglia. But he also had the most intimate connexions with London. These were military-cum-feudal since, as lord of Baynard's Castle, Fitzwalter was the city of London's *procurator*, hereditary standard-bearer and leader of the city militia. Beyond that, with his heavy involvement in the wine-trade, his links were economic as well and together they generated a closely woven web of contacts and favours, all of which he now seems to have called in.

The king was bidding for the support of the city as well and on 7 May he granted London a new charter. The charter confirmed the citizens' traditional liberties and gave them the right to elect a new mayor every year. It was a substantial concession. But it was not enough to eradicate the memory of John's heavy taxation and a faction of leading citizens plotted to surrender the city to the rebels.

Fitzwalter was in on the game and the rebel army marched overnight from Ware. They arrived early on the morning of Sunday, 17 May. They found the gates open and 'entered the city without any tumult while the inhabitants were performing divine service'. Fitzwalter and Mandeville took control: the property of the king's supporters was plundered and the houses of the Jews demolished and used as building materials to strengthen the city's defences.

The fall of London, 'the capital of the crown and the realm', was decisive. The royal administration broke down. Waverers and fence-sitters among the baronage, who had been many, saw which way the wind was blowing and came over to the rebels in droves. And any who held out were threatened with war against their persons and possessions. It was a brave – or calculating – man who resisted.

It took John less than ten days to bow to the inevitable.

On 27 May a truce was agreed and intermediaries were appointed on both sides. On 31 May the king took up residence at Windsor, where, with the exception of a brief absence in early June, he remained till the end of the month.

And on 10 June he came to Runnymede.

FIVE

RUNNYMEDE

Runnymede

Actually, most of the documents only talk of 'a meadow between Windsor and Staines'. But there is little or no doubt that they mean Runnymede. Runnymede is a meadow or 'mead' on the south bank of the River Thames, which was then principal highway of southern England. And it is conveniently situated between Windsor, where the king had his camp in the magnificent, almost impregnable castle, and Staines, where the barons, whose principal stronghold was in London some twenty miles to the east, had made their forward base.

But places between two armed camps, each bitterly mistrustful of the other, risk turning into battlefields. Runnymede was chosen precisely because it could not do so, as the surrounding land was too wet and boggy.

By early June the pace of negotiations was quickening and agreement was in sight. A week earlier, John's safe-conducts had referred only to intermediaries coming 'to treat concerning peace'; now they spoke of the baronial agents as authorised 'to make and secure peace'. Hence John's visit to Runnymede on 10 June. Accompanied by Stephen Langton, Archbishop of Canterbury, who had been the chief go-between between the king and the barons, John came to set his seal – literally – on the terms demanded by his magnates.

By an extraordinary chance, the very document survives. Headed 'These are the Articles which the barons seek and which the king agrees', it is a snapshot of a particular moment in time. The barons' negotiators have submitted a point-by-point shopping list of their demands. Like most such memoranda, the Articles are tersely written in portrait form; each demand starts on a fresh line and its beginning is marked by a pilcrow or paraph sign thus: '¶'.

We have encountered such a document before, when the barons drew up their terms at Brackley. According to Wendover, the document was arranged in the same fashion as the Articles, in *capitula* or 'heads'; and the barons had likewise demanded that the king signal his agreement by sealing it.

Then John had refused in anger and with contempt. Now was very different. Did he cavil to the bitter end? Or did he capitulate? We do not know. But agree he did. And to show that he really had agreed to the Articles, he did what the barons demanded and ordered his seal, the double-sided great seal of England, to be attached by the usual cords at the bottom.

There was a bitter irony about this. The seal had been the key instrument of Angevin power. It was deliberately large and impressive and it had carried the king's image and with it his authority to the furthest corners of his far-flung dominions. The design of the seal also made an important point about the nature of kingship. On the front the king is seated in majesty, as lawgiver and judge. On the reverse he is mounted and armed like a knight, as warrior-defender of his people.

The result is a visual representation of the most important single Old Testament text on kingship, in which the Jews defy the prophet Samuel and demand to have a king: 'that we may also be like all the nations and that our king may judge us, and go out before us and fight our battles' (I Samuel 8:19–20). The most devastating charge against John was that he had failed in both these fundamental, God-ordained duties of kingship: that he was an unjust judge and a cowardly, unchivalrous and above all unsuccessful knight.

That the seal was now used, as it would be too on Magna Carta itself, to surrender royal power and not to advance it, confirmed the damning verdict on John, his kingship, his government and the man himself.

The Articles were the work of the barons and they made no bones about the fact. They embodied their abiding concerns for the security of their lands, their widows and their heirs against John's arbitrary money-grabbing and they gave these matters pride of place. But they were much more. They were evidence of the rapidly changing politics of 1215 and, in particular, they testified to the collapse in the king's position. The 'unknown charter', which had seemed a *ne plus ultra* less than a month previously, contained only a dozen concessions; the Articles multiplied this figure fourfold to forty-eight.

The Articles also registered how far the barons had had to go in appealing to a much wider 'national' constituency. London, in particular, had done very well out of its decision – however taken – to back the barons rather than the king. The Articles offer guarantees of the liberties of the City and freedom of trade and navigation on the Thames and Medway; they also provide for reformed weights and measures through-out the kingdom – not forgetting of course measures of wine for Fitzwalter's friends among the vintners and in the victual-ling trade. More altruistically, the Articles also include a reworked version of the king's promise of 10 May about justice, which now takes up two articles. But, because this promise no longer had the strategic significance it held previ-ously, it loses its primacy: from first in the Unknown Charter to twenty-ninth and thirtieth in the Articles (and thirty-ninth and fortieth in Magna Carta itself).

But as striking – and as eloquent – is what the Articles silently omit or actively seek to exclude. Despite Fitzwalter's grandiose title of 'marshal of the army of God and Holy Church', the Articles make no mention whatever of the rights of the Church and they try – very firmly – to keep the Holy Father out of English politics. John, the last and most elaborately drafted article requires, shall:

procure nothing from the lord pope whereby any of the things here agreed might be revoked or diminished, and if he does procure any such thing, let it be reckoned void and null and let him make no use of it.

Security for the king's good behaviour on this point was to be given by charters of Langton, his fellow bishops and Pandulf, the papal legate himself!

The Articles, sealed with the king's great seal, were taken back to London by the barons' negotiators. Not surprisingly, in view of John's notorious unreliability, some of the barons refused to accept even the sealed document as earnest of the king's good faith. Most did, however, and the machinery set in motion by his sealing continued to turn. From the beginning it had been envisaged that the Articles would be incorporated into a charter and the first article makes pointed mention of the fact:

After the death of their predecessor, heirs who are of full age shall have their inheritance on payment of the old relief, *which is to be stated in the charter.*

Five days later on 15 June 1215 all was ready and John and his barons met again at Runnymede in plenary session.

The date is one of the most famous in English history,

celebrated by textbooks, politicians and campaigners as *the* date when Magna Carta was signed. Sculptors, painters and engravers have represented the event with every degree of elaboration and embellishment; Rudyard Kipling versified it; Churchill pontificated about it; there have even been calls to make 'Magna Carta Day' a Bank Holiday.

What historical 'fact' could be more certain? In fact almost everything that is supposed to have happened at Runnymede on 15 June is disputable or – still worse – unknowable.

John did not *sign* the charter. There is no evidence he could write and in any case in the twelfth century royal documents were not authenticated with the royal sign manual or signature but – as we have seen – with a seal. Probably indeed there was not even an engrossed charter available to seal (or sign) on 15 June. No original sealed copy of Magna Carta survives and there is no evidence that one ever existed. Even the date is in doubt. Only one chronicler gives 15 June as the date of the Charter and he probably derived it retrospectively, from the dating clause which the chancery clerks assigned to the Charter:

Given by our hand in the meadow which is called Runnymede between Windsor and Staines on the fifteenth day of June, in the seventeenth year of our reign.

Nevertheless the dating clause – adhered to in all known copies of the Charter – does suggest that something important was felt to have happened on the 15th – and at Runnymede. But what? Once again, the eventual text of the Charter offers the best clue.

'Wherefore', the concluding chapter 63 begins:

Wherefore we wish and firmly enjoin that the English church shall be free, and that the men in our kingdom shall have and hold all the aforesaid liberties, rights and concessions well and peacefully, freely and quietly, fully and completely, for themselves and their heirs from us and our heirs, in all matters and in all places for ever, as is aforesaid. *An oath, moreover, has been taken, as well on our part as on the part of barons, that all these things aforesaid shall be observed in good faith and without evil dispositions.*

In other words, what Kipling's 'reeds at Runnymede' should have remembered was not 'the curt uncompromising "sign"', but rather a proclamation and an oath-taking. First, in the face of the whole huge gathering, hundreds strong, of his bishops and barons, John had proclaimed his commitment to the gist of the Charter; then both sides – the king for his part and the barons for theirs – had solemnly sworn binding oaths: the king that he would issue Magna Carta and keep to it and the barons that they would (re)swear fealty in return.

Four days later, on 19 June, the king and his barons met once more at Runnymede. The previous confrontations there seem to have been business-like and often tense. In contrast, the 19th saw an occasion of high ceremony. Earlier in the year, as negotiations for a charter had broken down, the barons had renounced their allegiance to the king. Now, with the confirmation of the Charter guaranteed as surely as God and man could make it, the barons renewed their fealty. The king wore the imperial robes and regalia of his grandmother, the Empress Matilda; the barons knelt and swore individually.

Meanwhile, the clerks of the chancery had got down to work. They began by drawing up the Charter in proper diplomatic form. The rough shopping list of the Articles of the Barons was reworked into the smooth, continuous, densely written prose of the royal chancery. The text was made politer as the peremptory demands of the Articles were turned into the customary expressions of royal grace – 'we will', 'we grant', etc. – and it became much wordier as everything was fleshed out into full, unambiguous legal form.

At some stage between John's agreement to the Articles of the Barons on the 10th and the solemn rite of proclamation and oath-taking on the 15th, a few entirely new provisions had also been added. Some of them were very important, like the eventual chapter 14 of Magna Carta, which defined the 'common council' of the realm. The

Articles had required such 'common council' to agree to taxation. Chapter 14 defined the vague phrase to mean a properly summoned parliament-like assembly of bishops, barons and other major landlords.

Even more important – at least symbolically – is chapter 1 of the final Magna Carta by which John guaranteed for himself and his successors that 'the Church of England shall be free'. A version of this clause – 'in the first place (I) make the Holy Church of God free' – had appeared at the head of Henry I's coronation charter. But the barons had not included the demand in their Articles. Perhaps this was deliberate. The Articles are exclusively secular in their concerns and even – in the attempt to exclude a papal annulment of the settlement – tinged with anti-clericalism. More likely, however, the barons simply thought that the Church was well able to look after herself.

And, with Langton – cardinal, archbishop and eminent academic theologian – in charge of the negotiations between the king and the baronage, they were right.

Even so, chapter 1 of Magna Carta still surprises. It might take its key phrase from Henry I's charter. But it gave it an entirely new and topical gloss. Henry I had given the Church *financial* freedom, by promising not to take the income of bishoprics or abbeys during vacancies. Chapter 1 of Magna Carta, on the other hand, sought to give the Church *political* freedom, by guaranteeing it freedom of election to its senior posts.

Above all, it grounds the freedom of the Church differently — chronologically, logically and biographically. 'We wish (the freedom of the church) thus observed', John is made to declare:

> which is evident from the fact that, *before the quarrel between us and our barons began, we willingly and spontaneously* granted and by our charter [issued in November 1214] confirmed the freedom of elections . . . and obtained confirmation of it from the lord pope Innocent III [in January 1215].

It is hard to exaggerate the importance of all this. Langton — for there can be no doubt that the drafting is his — is declaring that the freedom granted to the Church is not only *different* from the liberties obtained by the barons, it is also *superior* because it is untainted by coercion. John had given the Church its freedom of his own free will; the barons, at every stage, had extorted their liberties either by the threat or the reality of force.

With a king like John, the barons of course had no choice. As events abundantly demonstrated, it was force or nothing. Nevertheless, the dilemma remained: as lawyers and moralists agreed, extorted consent is no consent.

Langton recognised the dilemma; deplored it and sought to rescue the Church from its horns. But he did so at the risk of detaching the Church from the political fabric of England.

Nevertheless – and in spite of these additions, however important – Magna Carta is essentially what the Articles made it. Which means that it is a document for its own time, not for ours. Even in its most famous, most apparently universal clauses like chapters 39 and 40:

> No free man shall be arrested or imprisoned or disseised or outlawed or exiled or in any way victimised, neither will we attack him or send anyone to attack him, except by the lawful judgment of his peers or by the law on the land . . . To no one will we sell, to no one will we refuse or delay right or justice.

These are clauses that would resonate through the ages; that still retain their power to quicken the blood; that even today remain word-for-word active and unrepealed on the statute book. But even they are not quite as gloriously far-reaching as we like to think. Clause 39 is *not* the origin of Habeas Corpus. It is not even the origin of trial by jury, since back in 1215 guilt or innocence in criminal matters was established, not by the verdict of a jury, but by trial by ordeal or by battle.

It is also worth reminding ourselves that these clauses owe their origin, not to the barons, but to John's declaration of 10 May 1215. This was a product of the same manufactory of fine words as the king's inaugural 'Constitution' and, by itself, meant just as little. Is this the clue to their survival? Not that their meaning is universal, as we like to assume. But that, as John Gillingham is more or less alone in daring to say, they are 'vague' and finally without much meaning at all?

Nevertheless, when historical revisionism has done its worst, there *is* something here that matters. The detail – Habeas Corpus, trial by jury – may be wrong. But the sense that Magna Carta defines and protects those three fundamental freedoms of the Anglo-Saxon world – life, liberty and property – is right.

And everything else flows from that.

SIX

FOR ALL AND FOR EVER

Scribe at work

At least as important as the content of Magna Carta is its intended scope. The Charter had been extorted from John by a baronial faction under threat of civil war. But it aspired to be something bigger and better: an agreement, no less, between the king and his whole people – all of them, or at least all of them who were 'free men'. And not only in 1215, but for all time. The resulting intergenerational compact was set out in sweepingly far-reaching terms in chapter 1:

> We have also granted to all free men of our kingdom, for ourselves and our heirs for ever, all the liberties written below, to be had and held by them and their heirs, of us and ours heirs.

The words 'all' and 'for ever' are easily written. But something that was intended to affect everybody and for all time had to be known everywhere and by everybody too. That would be a challenge now. It is astonishing how far it was accomplished then. That it was possible at all was a product – ironically – of John's own aggressive approach to government. It was this aggression which had provoked the crisis in the first place. But it had also created one of the most impressive pieces of administrative machinery in Europe: the English chancery.

The chancery was the royal writing office. And since England, more than most places at the time, was ruled by the written word, the chancery lay at the very heart of the king's government and followed his every movement. Not that we need suppose the king himself to be literate. Instead, like most of the warrior class, he most likely could neither read nor write but gave his instructions orally and in French. The chancellor and his staff of skilled clerks then turned these orders into Latin and – to prove they really were the king's – authenticated them by attaching the king's great seal.

Such sealed letters or 'writs' from the chancery communicated the king's commands not only to his subjects but also to the rest of the governmental machine. They ordered the exchequer to spend money, the judges to hear cases, commanders to raise troops and the sheriffs to carry out their multiple tasks in law enforcement and running the local government of the shires. Letters from the chancery also effected grants of office or land and recorded the terms of the numerous bargains into which the king entered with his subjects great and small, and with institutions, like monasteries, as well as individuals. The most authoritative of these agreements took the special form – like Magna Carta itself – of *charters* and were especially valued as binding the king and his successors.

All this business had increased piecemeal and pell-mell in the century or more since the Conquest, with each king making his particular contribution. Henry I developed the exchequer, Henry II the king's justice while Richard I's heady crusading ambitions and their eventual failure multiplied military and financial business. The result was that a trickle of writs became a torrent. Richard is supposed to have sent out two hundred writs to raise troops on a single night; the number of legal writs to the judges and sheriffs must often have been not far behind.

John and his great chancellor Hubert Walter reduced the resulting avalanche of parchment to order. They began the regular dating of letters by the 'regnal year' or year of the king's reign – as we have seen with Magna Carta itself, which was issued 'on the fifteenth day of June, in the seventeenth year of our reign'. John's seventeenth year ran from 28 May 1215 to 19 May 1216, so the 15th of June of this regnal year fell in the modern calendar year 1215.

The irregular length of John's regnal year was an additional complication. At this time, and indeed until the end of the fourteenth century, the date of the monarch's coronation was treated as his accession day, since he was not regarded as being fully king until he had been anointed and crowned. But John's coronation day fell on 27 May 1199, Ascension Day. Ascension Day is a moveable feast, which means that John's subsequent regnal years – running from

Ascension Day to Ascension Day – start and end on different calendar dates for each regnal year.

It all seems intolerably complicated. But, in the absence of any other agreed method of calculating time, it was an enormous step forward. As was the practice, also introduced by John and Hubert Walter, of registering chancery letters by 'enrolling' – that is copying – them onto great rolls of parchment. One roll was established for each principal category of business; and new rolls were started for each regnal year.

None of this was done for altruistic reasons of course. Quite the opposite. John was congenitally disposed to mistrust his subjects and to believe – in the absence of irrefutable evidence to the contrary – that they were trying to pull wool over his eyes. The enrolments provided the king with the necessary evidence of authenticity. But they also, whatever John intended, provided his subjects with a similar security against his own vagaries.

The royal will, like the date, was becoming a known and knowable thing.

All this was achieved with pen, ink and parchment, by hand and with no mechanical help whatever. Such prodigious productivity was possible only because of the quasi-military discipline of the chancellor and his clerks. There were plentiful supplies of parchment, made from scraped, stretched and dried sheepskin; of pens, made from goose quills; and of ink, which, manufactured from iron and extract of oak galls and thickened with gum arabic, was dark, lustrous and indelible. The writs were mostly short, terse and formulaic. The clerks were well schooled and wrote Latin quickly in a heavily abbreviated, standard 'chancery' hand.

But the real key was the use of dictation. Dictation was used to copy writs and letters onto the rolls; it also facilitated the production of multiple copies of the same document – like Magna Carta.

John, with that occasional, driving energy which was one aspect of his complex, contradictory character, had begun with a vigorous show of implementing the Charter promptly and in full. While still at Runnymede on the 19th, he ordered the issue of 'writs', or formal royal orders under the great seal, commanding the sheriffs and other royal officials to set in motion the Charter and the projected grand resolution of disputes between the king and his subjects of which the Charter was the centrepiece. The sheriffs were to swear obedience to the Committee of Twenty-Five which had been set up to oversee the detailed implementation of the Charter; to impanel juries to enquire into 'evil customs' and claims of royal misgovernment; and to arrange for public readings of the Charter throughout the country.

The 'Magna Carta' writs of 19 June were of course a one-off and, at about two hundred and fifty words, significantly longer than usual. Even so, within the week copies seem to have been despatched to all the counties: the first batch of twenty-one on or soon after the 19th, and a further fourteen on or about the 24th. All this is impressive and shows both the chancery and the new machinery of enrol-ment (which alone records all this) at their best.

But the distribution of the Charter itself, without which the enforcement of the writs was difficult if not impossible, was slower and much more patchy. The first six copies were not handed over till the 24th and it took almost a month to produce another seven. That gives a total of only thirteen in all, which would have covered just over a third of the counties. Moreover – despite the claims of monastic chron-iclers and some modern authorities – there is no conclusive evidence than any others were made.

No doubt the length of the Charter told against it. A writ of a couple of hundred words could be knocked out in an hour or two from start to finish. But a four-thousand-word document, like the Charter, was a very different matter. It took a skilled clerk days, not hours. It filled a whole membrane or skin of parchment, rather than the few-inch-wide strip needed for a writ. And it was correspondingly costly.

In view of this, it is possible that copies of Magna Carta were made only for those who demanded them – and were prepared to pay. Which would of course explain why so few survive. Or it could be that even the well-oiled machinery of the chancery was overwhelmed by the sudden burden of work. But the most likely explanation is simply that the painstaking process of copying was overtaken by events. By the time the second batch of seven Charters was ready for distribution on 22 July, the fragile peace between John and his barons had begun to break down and Magna Carta itself was on the way to being a dead letter.

Why go to further trouble in reproducing a now irrelevant document?

SEVEN

FAILURE

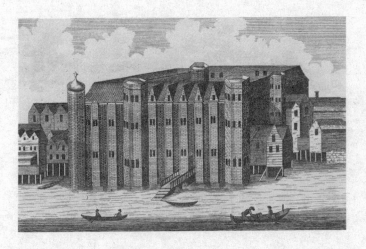

Baynard's Castle, London

Traditionally, the king is saddled with the entire blame for the failure of Magna Carta. Actually, whatever his private feelings may have been, John's initial public attitude was impeccable. His baronial opponents, on the other hand, quickly proved to be truculent, grasping and as irresponsible in their new-found power as John at his worst.

But the real problem lay elsewhere: not in personal foibles, but in the complex and unstable geometry of the Runnymede settlement. For so much more had happened in those heady June days than we think. Magna Carta itself was a multifarious thing, and was designed, not only as a statement of rights and liberties, but also as a mechanism to redress the wrongs of John's government and prevent their recurrence. In addition, John and his barons had entered into a formal treaty about the possession of London, while the barons had also given a solemn, witnessed undertaking about their good faith. All this is on the record. But heaven knows how much else was off: how many handshakes, nudges, nods and winks, how many under-the-table deals.

Even Langton, with his academic punctiliousness, must have found it hard to keep track.

Taking everything together, however, it all seemed to guarantee 'the firm peace . . . made by the grace of God between us and our barons', which John had announced to the kingdom in his letters patent despatched – in the first flush of hope – from Runnymede on 18 and 19 June. But there was a dangerous, and it turned out fatal, asymmetry between the various elements. Put crudely, the barons had John over a barrel. John, in contrast, only had the barons' word.

And it proved so much wind.

The barons had bitter personal experience of John's systematic dishonesty. They knew he would try to wriggle out of the Charter and they were determined to stop him. The result was the *forma securitatis*. This was the most revolutionary provision of Magna Carta and – to its last word – it was directly and solely the barons' own work.

The fact is evident from the draft of the Charter known as the Articles of the Barons. Almost all the individual articles, as we have seen, are brief, one-line notes. They sketch the substance of a demand whose detailed drafting the barons were content to leave to the practised hands of royal chancery clerks. Not so the *forma securitatis*. Here the barons would trust nobody but themselves. They made it the last and culminating of the Articles. It was the only 'head' they had written out in detail and in full in a long paragraph of continuous prose. And it was the only one incorporated *in extenso* and with scarcely a word changed into the published text of Magna Carta.

It is easy to see why.

Headed 'this is the *forma securitatis* ("formula or terms of security") for the preservation of the peace and liberties between the king and the kingdom', it set up a panel of twenty-five barons. The Twenty-five were to be chosen by the baronage 'as they wish'; and they were given far-reaching powers: 'with all their might . . . to observe, maintain and cause to be observed the peace and liberties which we have granted'. Any breach of the Charter, whether by the king or by his officials, was to be notified to any four of the panel. If the breach were not rectified within forty days, the four were to refer the matter to the Twenty-five and the Twenty-five in turn, 'with the commune of all the land', were authorised to 'distrain and distress Us in every way they can, namely by seizing castles, lands and possessions' until, 'in their judgment', the king had made amends. In other words, under the cloak of the legal process of distraint, the *forma securitatis* authorised the Twenty-five to bring the king to heel by levying war upon him. His own person, and those of the queen and his children, were to be spared. Otherwise nothing was to be off limits.

The Twenty-five were to be the sole judge of the proportionality of their actions. Everyone, willy-nilly, was to swear to obey them and to assist them 'in distressing us to the best of their ability'. If any of the Twenty-five were to die, another was to be chosen in his place. The majority were empowered to act on behalf of the whole body and overrule absentees or dissenters. And they were all bound by a mutual oath.

In other words, the Twenty-five were a genuine committee of public safety. They were designed to be permanent and, in the process of time, they would have become a self-recruiting aristocratic oligarchy and turned England into a Venetian republic with the king as its puppet doge.

It was not to be. But the Twenty-five also had an immediate purpose which they served to great effect. The Charter, operating on the premiss that the king was in the wrong and the barons were in the right, had provided for comprehensive redress and compensation by the king: all John's additions to the forest were to be disafforested; 'all hostages and charters delivered to Us . . . as securities for peace or faithful service' were to be given back; 'any one . . . disseised or deprived by Us without lawful judgment of his peers' was to have his rights and property restored; all unlawful or excessive fines were to be remitted.

And all of this was to be done *statim*: 'at once'. The word echoes through the final chapters of Magna Carta like a death-knell for royal power. Which was of course the intention.

But what gave these demands for compensation teeth were the powers of the Twenty-five. They were the judges of the facts of each case and the assessors of the adequacy of John's compensation. It would be hard think of a more outrageously prejudiced tribunal. They included in their ranks many of the most prominent casualties of John's misgovernment; and they acted as judge, jury, prosecutor – and indeed executioner – rolled into one.

Finally, like most revolutionary tribunals, the Twenty-five revelled in their new-found power to humiliate their former persecutor. The *forma securitatis* had stipulated that, in case of complaint, the four representative members of the Twenty-five should 'come to Us' to state their case. This proved to be beneath the barons' dignity and instead the king, stricken with gout, was carried on a litter into the presence of the Twenty-five, who would neither excuse his presence nor do judgment in his chamber.

No wonder John's foreign mercenaries are supposed to have scoffed that he had been reduced to 'the twenty-fifth king in England . . . not now a king, nor even a petty king, but a disgrace to kings'.

This was pure *force majeure*. It was applied brutally and with calculation, just as John had done in his days of power. And it had the desired effect as John rushed to meet the claims against him. Fifty were settled in the ten days alone following the ending of the Runnymede meeting on 19 June. The Twenty-five did especially well with twelve of their number benefiting from the bonanza. Richard de Clare got

Buckingham, Robert Fitzwalter Hertford Castle, and Henry de Bohun the manors of the honour of Trowbridge. John occasionally demurred. On 23 June he referred a claim by Geoffrey de Mandeville, Earl of Essex, to the local sheriffs for investigation. But, later the same day and in the face of pressures we can only guess at, the king backed down and made the grant anyway.

John's prostration in the aftermath of Runnymede was real enough. He was a king *sans* everything: without power, without respect, and – what was arguably worst of all – without a capital. As we have seen, it was the barons' seizure of London in the brief civil war of May 1215 which had forced John to his capitulation at Runnymede. Magna Carta itself studiously avoided the issue: both as being too injurious to the king's dignity and too honest about the origins of the Charter. Instead, the custody of the city was dealt with separately, in one of the most remarkable and most humiliating documents to be sealed by an English king.

Calling itself a *conventio* ('pact' or 'treaty'), it records an agreement between 'the Lord John, king of England', *ex una parte* ('on the one part') and 'Robert Fitzwalter, marshal of the army of God and Holy Church in England', his fellow members of the Twenty-five and 'other earls, barons and free men of the whole kingdom' *ex altera parte* ('on the other part'), about the custody of London. The barons, under the fig-leaf of being the king's bailiffs, would retain possession of the city and Tower of London until 15

August. If the king had fulfilled the specified conditions by then, the city and Tower would be handed back. And if not, not.

The agreement was written out twice on a membrane of parchment about ten inches wide and eighteen inches long. The two copies were separated by an irregular, wavy cut; one copy, sealed by the king, was given to the barons; the other copy, sealed by the barons, was retained by the king. And it is the latter copy which survives in The National Archives.

This kind of document is known as an 'indenture'. The name comes from the 'teeth' left by the irregular cut which severed the two original identical copies. In case of dispute, the two copies could be reunited: if the 'teeth' tallied exactly, the documents were authentic; if not, one or other had been tampered with. This simple form of security made the indenture immensely popular; it became the most common form of contract between the king's subjects and it was used for everything, from land-sales to apprenticeship agreements.

But this was the only time it was used to decide the possession of London.

And that was not the only remarkable thing about the document. Not only did it treat London in effect as a piece of private property; it also treated the king as a private person. Or, at the very least, it reduced him from a sovereign to the contractual equal of a supposedly representative group of his subjects. And scarcely even the equal in fact. For, as throughout the Runnymede settlement, the terms of the agreement were heavily weighted against the king.

In one sense, this was no more than a recognition of brute fact: possession is nine-tenths of the law and the barons were in possession of London. They would not lightly give it up. The indenture spelled out their conditions in careful, pedantic detail: 'within the agreed term' (that is, by 15 August), the oath to the Twenty-five was to have been administered throughout England; local commissions of twelve knights were to have been sworn in to investigate misconduct by sheriffs and abuses in the forest law; and the king was to have met all claims against him for the restoration of rights and property, whether admitted by him or adjudicated by the Twenty-five.

All this, of course, established not only conditions but a timetable – and a tight one at that. The indenture, which had teeth in more senses of the word than one, gave John two months exactly from the Runnymede agreement on 15 June to the deadline of 15 August to fulfil the initial, basic requirements of Magna Carta.

Otherwise his loss of both the City and Tower of London risked becoming permanent.

It is now easy to see why John made such haste to put the Magna Carta settlement into effect. He had no choice. But there was also calculation in it. Royalist support had been reduced to a rump. But the revolutionary zealots of the Twenty-five were a minority also. Between these extremes lay the great body of English opinion. The better John behaved, and was seen to behave, the more chance he had of winning it over.

And so it proved. Within a few weeks, the Twenty-five, hitherto so imperiously confident, were looking over their shoulders. The result was a remarkable letter, written in early July, from their leader, Robert Fitzwalter, 'marshal of the army of God and Holy Church in England', to a fellow member of the Twenty-five, William d'Aubigny of Belvoir. The Twenty-five were politicians but they were soldiers first. And, cooped up in London, they and their men were getting bored. To relieve the tedium, they had arranged a tournament to be held at Stamford on 6 July. Stamford, on the borders of Lincolnshire and Northamptonshire, lay in the heartlands of baronial support. But it was a hundred miles from London and an event there risked denuding the city of its garrison.

In the first flush of their triumph at Runnymede, the Twenty-five had thought the risk negligible; now, only three weeks later, they were not so sure: 'Be it known to you as a fact', Fitzwalter wrote to d'Aubigny, 'that we have been forewarned that there are some who are only waiting for our departure from the city to take possession of it on a sudden.' To prevent this catastrophe, the tournament had been moved to the purlieus of London, on the heath between

Staines and Hounslow. D'Aubigny was warmly encouraged to come 'well provided with horses and arms, that you may there obtain honour'.

As an added inducement, he was informed of the victor's prize: 'whoever performs well there will receive a bear which a lady will send to the tournament'.

It made a change, I suppose, from baiting the king.

Meanwhile John's room for political manoeuvre – and with it his confidence – rose as the Twenty-five's diminished. Before the Runnymede meeting broke up, it was agreed that the two sides together with the bishops should reconvene at Oxford on 16 July to review outstanding business. The date seems to have been carefully chosen as the halfway point of the two-month timetable laid down by the London *conventio*. The meeting also saw the king retake the political initiative for the first time. Unable to make the first day of the session, he sent a high-powered group of representatives: 'they are to do for you', he informed the Twenty-five, 'what we ought to do for you, and to receive from you what you ought to do for us'.

This demand for reciprocity was cleverly chosen. It called attention to John's good faith in taking the many steps he had so far towards fulfilling the Charter. It justified him in taking no more until the Twenty-five showed matching good faith. And it set a trap for the barons which they walked right into.

As we have seen, the barons at Runnymede had given the king a solemn, witnessed undertaking

> they had promised the lord king that whatsoever form of security he wished to have from them to observe the peace, they would let him have it, apart from giving him castles and hostages.

John was astute enough to call the promise in at Oxford. And the barons were foolish enough to renege on it. So blatantly in fact that Langton and the bishops felt obliged to offer public written testimony to the fact. Their statement recorded the barons' original pledge at Runnymede, made 'in our presence and hearing'; confirmed that in fulfilment of their promise John had required them to make charters confirming their allegiance; and reported the barons' blank refusal: 'they would not do it'.

Oxford was an important public relations victory for John. A new picture was emerging of a well-intentioned king confronted by a faction of overweening and devious aristocratic *frondeurs*. The picture neatly stood the barons' propaganda about John on its head. It would of course have been ludicrously implausible only a few months previously. But the Twenty-five's intransigent behaviour seemed to give it substance.

John, always a shrewd tactician, recognised a good line when he saw it and assiduously harped on the theme. His next opportunity came at the meeting, once again at Oxford, which began the day after the expiry of the deadline of 15 August. John did not appear in person but his envoys were instructed to say that he

> had surrendered many things as he had agreed, but that he had received nothing in return since the peace, except grave injuries and tremendous damages which had been inflicted on him and which no one was ready to amend.

He even claimed to be in fear of his life: 'it would be neither safe nor wise for him to make himself available . . . since they had gathered together in arms and in such numbers'.

It was not his fault, he protested, that the Runnymede settlement was not going forward as planned.

This meeting, and a follow-up at Staines at the end of the month, was to be the last time that the king and the Twenty-five met in quasi-peace. Instead, within days, the political scene was transformed by the news that John had appealed to Rome.

EIGHT

ROMAN ECHOES

Rome

Communications between England and Rome were like a gigantic echo chamber. A report would be sent from England. Then, two months or more later, a reply would come from Rome – imperious, orotund, minatory – like a mighty, long-delayed, much-distorted echo, awesome in its sonorousness and sometimes in its effects.

So it was in the autumn of 1215. Innocent III, preoccupied with the preparations for the General Council of the Church which he had summoned to meet at the Lateran in November 1215, had remained in ignorance of the summer's tumultuous events in his far-away fiefdom of England. He knew of course of the dispute between John and his barons and in March he had sent his *triplex forma pacis* to all three parties: the king, the barons and Archbishop Langton. In the *triplex forma pacis* the pope had spoken both *ex cathedra* and as sovereign and he naturally expected it to settle the matter. He was therefore outraged when in early July he received John's letters of 29 May. The letters, written on the eve of Runnymede, told of the barons' renunciation of their allegiance and their capture of London. And they implied that both were in express defiance of Innocent's injunctions in the *triplex forma pacis*. These had ordered the barons, under pain of excommunication, to desist from their violent leagues and conspiracies; to make their requests of the king with due regard to his royal honour and to leave coercion, were it necessary, to the pope as overlord.

This was enough for Innocent. The barons had defied him. Langton and the bishops had failed to excommunicate them. Both must be taught obedience. The lesson was administered in the bull *Mirari cogimur et moveri* ('We are compelled to wonder and be moved') of 7 July. King John, 'our well beloved son in Christ', Innocent began, had given 'satisfaction beyond what we expected to God and the church'. Why then had Langton and his fellow bishops not reciprocated by extending the protection of the Church to him as commanded in the *triplex forma pacis*? How could they be so indifferent to 'the business of the Holy Cross (the Crusade), the mandate of the Apostolic See and their oath of fealty'? Was it, he insinuated, that they were 'cognisant of, not to say associates in, this wicked conspiracy'? For let there be no doubt, Innocent continued, the barons were 'undoubtedly worse than Saracens, since they endeavour to expel from his kingdom him who it was rather hoped would afford assistance to the Holy Land'.

The clerks of the papal chancery now opened the diapason stop on their rhetoric: 'We', the bull thundered:

on behalf of the omnipotent God the Father, and the Son, and the Holy Ghost, and by the authority of the

apostles Peter and Paul, and by our own authority, lay
the fetters of excommunication on all these disturbers
of the king and kingdom or England, as well as on all
their accomplices and abettors . . . and place their
possessions under the ecclesiastical interdict.

Innocent then ordered the archbishop and bishops, 'by virtue
of their obedience', to proclaim this sentence of excommunication 'solemnly . . . throughout all England on every
Sunday and feast day amidst the ringing of bell and with
burning of candles'. If any bishop demurred, he was to be
suspended. There was to be no appeal.

Langton was aghast at the pope's intervention. From the
beginning, he had seen his role as mediator and moderator
between the king and the barons. Now he was commanded
to abandon his neutrality – which Innocent denounced as
'irresolution' or, still worse, complicity – and take sides
against the barons. Confronted with a direct papal order,
Langton had no choice and the excommunication of 'all
disturbers of the king and kingdom of England' was
proclaimed at the conference at Staines in late August. But
the unspecific and general terms of the excommunication
were greeted with derision. Some wags even dared to suggest
that, framed as loosely as it was, it could just as easily apply
to the king himself!

Beyond the general excommunication, however, Langton

was not prepared to go. He would obey the letter of Innocent's bull. He would go no further.

It was a forlorn gesture. Innocent had anticipated Langton's reaction and had entrusted the enforcement of the bull to three special commissioners: Peter des Roches, the curialist Bishop of Winchester, Pandulf, the papal legate, and the Abbot of Reading. They got to work immediately and published a letter on 5 September which dotted the i's and crossed the t's in the bull. The letter excommunicated the barons' leaders by name and specified their offences; it placed the city of London under interdict as being complicit in the barons' disobedience and it extended the sentence of excommunication to the barons' clerical associates. These included Giles, Bishop of Hereford (son and heir of the late favourite William de Briouze); William, Archdeacon of Hereford, who had been outlawed with Robert Fitzwalter after the assassination plot of 1212, Robert, 'chaplain of Robert Fitzwalter', and 'Alexander the clerk'.

Most of these clerics are mere names. But it was they surely who supplied the intellectual underpinning for the barons' case. They were their secretariat, translating their demands into Latin and putting them in proper form. They wrote their letters and propaganda; preached sermons on their behalf and maintained services in the London churches in defiance of the papal interdict.

And maybe 'Alexander the clerk' is more than a name. He has been plausibly identified as Master Alexander of St

Albans, surnamed Cementarius or 'The Mason' and a royal clerk. In the days of the Interdict, he was an ardent partisan of John and had advanced a series of controversial propositions. He elevated royal power 'declaring that the king was the rod of God and had been made a prince in order to rule his people . . . with a rod of iron, and to break them all "like a potter's vessel"'. Conversely, he attacked the foundations of papal authority, claiming 'that it was not the pope's business to meddle with the lay estates of kings . . . or with the government of their subjects; especially as nothing, except the power only over the church and church property, had been conferred by the Lord on St Peter.'

John rewarded him well for his writings, with benefices confiscated from churchmen who had remained loyal to the pope. After John's reconciliation with Innocent, Alexander was stripped of his ill-gotten gains and reduced to penury. In April 1215, John, now the pope's 'well beloved son in Christ', interceded with Innocent on Alexander's behalf in a remarkable, rhapsodical letter that sounds as though it was dictated by the 'pseudo-theologian' (as Wendover calls him) himself:

The lies [John is made to write] that were put upon Master Alexander of St Albans, our clerk, were circulated only by the breath of envy; wherefore it may be aptly said . . . that, as much was inflicted upon Isaiah by the Jewish people; upon Moses for the Ethiopian woman, and Paul for the Seven Churches, so was no less inflicted on Master Alexander by the slanderous rabble.

Heaven knows what Innocent made of this farrago, as the words 'Seven Churches' are written in the English vernacular!

Within a few weeks of the date of the letter, the world had been turned upside-down by the barons' revolt: John was now the pope's darling; the barons his increasingly bitter enemy. What more natural than for the Erastian and anti-papalist Alexander to trim his sails to the prevailing wind and put his rabble-rousing talents at the service of the barons? Indeed we can hear – almost to the word – his old arguments in Wendover's account of the contemptuous reception of the papal interdict in the city of London. It was rejected, he explains, partly because it had been obtained by false representations,

> but chiefly . . . because the management of lay affairs did not pertain to the pope, since the apostle Peter and his successors had only been entrusted by the Lord with the control and management of church matters.

Evidently royal power was not the only form of authority to be called into question in that revolutionary summer.

*

Innocent's bull and his commissioners' letter of 5 September marked the end of compromise – and Langton. Langton had been the centre of English politics ever since his return and the crisis of Magna Carta had only emphasised his role. But his refusal to go beyond the general excommunication and impose penalties on the named baronial leaders inevitably led to his suspension. The penalty was imposed by the Bishop of Winchester in mid-September. Langton appealed to Rome, where he had already arranged to go to attend the Lateran Council. In vain. Innocent confirmed Langton's suspension on 4 November and his career in church and state seemed destined to end in humiliation and failure.

By a final irony, Langton's departure from England more or less coincided with the arrival of a messenger from Rome at the end of September bearing another thunderous bull from Innocent III. Dated 24 August, the bull completed the work of the three papal commissioners by turning the papal ire on Magna Carta itself.

Innocent denounced the Charter as extorted 'by such violence and fear as might affect the most courageous of men'; declared it dishonourable to the Apostolic See, injurious to the king's rights, shameful to the English nation and seriously damaging to the projected Crusade; forbade John to keep his oath to observe it and the barons from any attempt to hold the king to his word; and condemned the Charter itself, finally and utterly, as *'null and void of all validity for ever'*.

Magna Carta was dead. It had died in vain. And it would never be resurrected. Or so the highest earthly authority in Christendom had declared.

John, it transpired, had asked Innocent to annul the Charter and release him from his oath as early as 22 June. His show of conformity over the summer had been a charade. But it had worked. He was no longer isolated. He had a party and a cause.

But so of course did the Twenty-five. They and their supporters were as deaf to the papal anathemas as John in the days of the Interdict. For them the Charter was alive and they would do anything to keep it so.

There were now two irreconcilable parties in England: the only upshot was war.

NINE

CIVIL WAR AND WAR OF WORDS

*Seal of Robert Fitzwalter, with the armorial shield
of his brother-in-arms, Saer de Quincy*

The first clash in the renewed civil war came quickly. Rochester, whose Norman cathedral and castle still stand much as they were in King John's day, occupied a vital strategic position. It straddled Watling Street, the Roman road that ran from Dover to London, and at its most vulnerable point where it crossed the fiercely tidal River Medway on a wooden bridge. Watling Street was John's lifeline: he could land men, mercenaries and munitions from his Continental territories and allies at Dover and move them via Watling Street to the rest of England.

But not if Rochester Castle were held against him.

Custody of the castle had been granted by Henry I to the archbishops of Canterbury. Naturally, in view of Langton's carefully maintained neutrality, John became nervous about its security. An agreement was reached with the archbishop that the castle should be transferred to royally nominated custodians as soon as peace was agreed in England. Magna Carta activated that condition and on 9 August John ordered Langton to hand Rochester over to the reliable Peter des Roches, Bishop of Winchester. Langton refused and at the end of September the castle was surrendered to the Twenty-five. Fortunately for his own skin,

Langton was already out of the country. But John never forgave him, denouncing him as 'a notorious and barefaced traitor to us, since he did not surrender Rochester to us in our so great need'.

The Twenty-five put a garrison in the castle, under the command of one of their own number, William d'Aubigny of Belvoir. John responded by occupying the city on 13 October with a much larger force and investing the castle. The royalist soldiers used the cathedral next door as a barracks, where they slept, ate, drank and even stabled their horses. Fitzwalter, d'Aubigny's friend, jousting companion and, as 'marshal of the army of God', military supremo of the Twenty-five, had sworn that the barons would come to his aid if he were besieged. Accordingly, on 26 October a force of 700 knights sallied out from London. But at Dartford, having heard that John was marching against them, they turned tail and retreated to their stronghold of London.

Left to himself, d'Aubigny held out for another five weeks, and it was not until 30 November that the exhaustion of supplies and the threat of starvation forced the garrison to surrender.

John had lost two vital months. But the barons had not covered themselves in glory either.

The war was also a war of words and ideas – centring, as always, on the Charter and, in particular, the extraordinary powers of the Twenty-five. These powers, as the three papal commissioners complained, had been used throughout the summer to diminish and control the king and usurp his proper, God-ordained authority:

> The dignity of the king has been stolen, since (the Twenty-five) grant out lands, a thing unheard of, and nullify the approved customs of the realm, and establish new laws, and destroy or alter all that has been prudently ordained by the king, their lord, with the advice of the magnates who were then his familiars.

The Twenty-five, the commissioners concluded, 'have gone as far as they could in despoiling the king of his royal dignity'.

In fact, far from being the worst the Twenty-five could do, this proved only to be the beginning as the events of the autumn drove to them to ever more extreme measures.

The first challenge came when John, aided and abetted by the pope, rejected the Charter. This drove the Twenty-five into a corner. They had gone too far to surrender. Their only hope was to overthrow John. Fitzwalter and de Vescy had tried this once before with the assassination plot of 1212. They tried it again now but sought to dignify the process by using the Charter as a machinery to legitimate deposition. Invoking the oath to the Twenty-five, they summoned a council to elect a new king. But the royalist magnates rejected the summons, declaring that 'they were not bound by oath to depose or expel the king, particularly since he had asserted his readiness to observe the agreed peace'.

Undeterred, the Twenty-five went ahead anyway and offered the crown to Prince Louis, the eldest son of Philip Augustus of France. Despite papal pressure, Louis accepted but failed to send any immediate help to the rebel barons. In the opinion of the Twenty-five there was now an interregnum. They filled the vacuum by using their powers to create a quasi-republic. They even clothed it with novel and daringly radical administrative forms.

The *forma securitatis* stated that any four members of the Twenty-five could refer a matter to the whole body for adjudication and action. The London barons made creative use of this provision to set up what looks like an executive committee. Two of the instructions it sent out survive. Issued in the name of three of the Twenty-five and witnessed by a fourth, they ostensibly seek to implement the decision of the Twenty-five to reinstate Nicholas de Stuteville in possession of Knaresborough Castle in Yorkshire.

One, addressed to the royal castellan, Brian de Lisle, informs him of the adjudication; commands him, on sight of their letters and by virtue of the oath which he had sworn 'to observe the common Charter of the realm', to give Stuteville possession of castle, 'which is adjudged to him as his right by the Twenty-five'; and threatens him with the consequences of disobedience: 'if you do not do this, you are henceforward at our peril, in body, lands and goods, since all who disobey this judgment are against the judgment and law of the realm'.

The other, in similar form, was addressed to Robert de Ros, himself a member of the Twenty-five, who was acting as 'custodian' or baronial sheriff of Yorkshire. He was ordered to muster his men, 'apart from those whom we shall order to come to us for the affairs of the realm', to aid de Stuteville 'by any and every means (*cum toto conamine*) in distraining and distressing the garrison of the castle'.

The words, *ad distringendum et ad gravandum*, are taken from the *forma securitatis* as it was incorporated in chapter 61 of Magna Carta. But the adherence to the letter of the Charter is a creative fiction. This in reality is an order from the Twenty-five's council of war to a regional commander about the deployment of troops in the coming civil war. De Ros was to besiege Knaresborough, while keeping a reserve in hand in case the Twenty-five needed reinforcements in London.

But the form of these two letters is as remarkable as their contents. They mimic a royal writ: they begin with a salutation (*salutem*); they issue a command (*mandamus*) and they end with a *teste* or authorising clause which gives the place where (*apud Londonias*) and the date when they were written. But even the date proclaims their singularity, since it is given, not as John's regnal year, but as 'the 30th day of September in the year of grace 1215'.

In other words, these are writs without a king and they are intended to usher in, however briefly, a world without kings also. They replace the oath of allegiance to the king with the oath to the Charter which, *ipso facto*, becomes a sort of sovereign constitution. The date is indeed 1215. But the mental universe these documents invoke is more familiar centuries hence, in the English Republic of the seventeenth century, or the Constitution of United States of the eighteenth. This is not time travel. The ideas were there in the Charter itself. And they germinated in months, not centuries, in the short-lived revolutionary regime of the Twenty-five.

TEN

DESPERATION

Newark Castle

By early 1216 the position of John's enemies was desperate and the king seemed to hold the advantage everywhere. He marched north, harrying the land as he went. The Yorkshire rebels fled before him into Scotland, which John invaded. He raided the lowlands, captured Berwick, Scotland's richest town, and burned it to the ground to punish Alexander II, King of Scots, for his support of the rebels. Then he struck south into the other main centre of disaffection, East Anglia, where he captured Colchester. As the defeated rebels were brought to heel, they had to swear an oath to renounce the Charter:

> I will not in any way hold to the Charter of liberties which the lord king has granted to the barons of England as a body and which the lord pope has annulled.

Both the revolutionary rule of the Twenty-five and Magna Carta itself faced oblivion.

The rebels' only hope was French intervention. They had already offered the crown to Prince Louis the previous autumn. Now, as they faced personal and political disaster, the two hard-line baronial leaders, Robert Fitzwalter and his blood-brother, Saer de Quincy, Earl of Winchester, went to France to renew the offer in person and beg for help before it was too late. At a council held at Melun in late April, Philip Augustus decided to ignore both his existing truce with John and vehement papal intervention in favour of the English king and allow his son to support the rebels.

Events quickly vindicated Philip's judgment as John's apparent supremacy collapsed like a house built on sand. His troops were mercenaries: they may have regained territory but their savagery had alienated support. Paying for them had also exhausted the last of John's money and the troubled state of the country made it next to impossible to raise any more. None of the rebel leaders had come over. Finally, and above all, John had never been strong enough to retake London.

Aware, it seems, of his own fundamental weakness, John failed to challenge Louis when he landed at Sandwich on 22 May with a powerful force. John fell back towards Winchester and the comfort of his palatial castle there; Louis marched straight for London. He entered the city on 2 June and, the following day, Fitzwalter and the mayor, William Handel, led the barons and citizens in doing homage to him as king in St Paul's Churchyard. Four days later, Louis left in hot pursuit of John.

The French prince, with his dramatic eruption into English politics, had fully lived up to his nickname of 'Louis the Lion'. But there was more to his success than mere military prowess. He came with carefully targeted propaganda as well. We can even guess the name of its author. Simon Langton was the younger brother of Archbishop Stephen Langton of Canterbury and, like him, was almost certainly a product of the Paris schools. Stephen had used him as his agent during the negotiations with John for his return from exile; after the ending of the Interdict, he became the archbishop's *chef de cabinet*, probably as his chancellor; and in 1215 he was himself elected Archbishop of York. But Innocent III quashed his election amid much acrimony.

As a calculated act of revenge, no doubt, Simon joined Louis' invasion of England as *his* chancellor – and, almost certainly, principal ideologue. The result was a carefully crafted claim to the throne which presented Louis, 'whether in regard to hereditary succession or to election . . . [as having] a most firm title to the realm of England'.

The 'firm title' was set out in narrative form in Louis' letter, written shortly after his landing, to the Abbot of St Augustine's, Canterbury. The letter began with the familiar territory of hereditary right. John, it argued, had forfeited any such right by his excommunication and formal disseising (or confiscation of his estates) by the justiciar and council for his treason to his absent brother Richard in 1194. With

John incapable of being Richard's heir, the succession passed in survivorship to Richard's sister, Eleanor, Queen of Castile, who had outlived all her other siblings and only died in 1214. Among many other offspring, Eleanor had a daughter Blanche, who married Prince Louis himself. In view of this marriage, Louis informed the abbot, Queen Eleanor 'freely conferred the right which she had in the realm [of England] on us and her daughter, whom we have as wife'.

This kind of farrago was par for the course with a pretender. It was better crafted than most, and more plausible, since it rested on *suppressio veri* rather than blatant *suggestio falsi*. It also showed a knowledge of English history which only a well-informed Englishman, like Simon Langton, could have possessed. No Frenchman could possibly have written it.

Otherwise, it was unremarkable.

Not so the second half of Louis' letter, which dealt with his claim to be King of England by election. Here we enter the world of the Charter, in which allegiance is not a given but a contract.

And it was a contract which, the letter claimed, John had broken twice over.

The first occasion came with his surrender of the realm to the pope. This action, which had been carried out 'without the advice and consent of his barons', was stated to be in clear breach of the oath which John 'swore solemnly at his coronation as the practice is to preserve the customs of both the church and realm of England . . . which was always free'.

The second occasion came with John's repudiation of his oaths at Runnymede. Following John's repeated misgovernment and after many petitions, the letter explained, 'war was levied against him by his barons'. As part of the settlement, 'it was agreed, by John's express consent, that, if he returned to his earlier wickedness, the barons should withdraw their allegiance'. Notoriously, the letter continued, and within a short time, John had broken his oath, 'seeking not only to oppress but rather wholly to exterminate' his barons.

In the circumstances, the barons, 'with the advice and approval of the "commune" of the realm [and] judging him unworthy of the realm, elected Us as king and lord'.

The first thing that strikes in this latter section of letter is that it embodies – much more than Magna Carta itself or even the Articles of the Barons – an exclusively baronial concept of politics. Their 'advice and consent' is the be-all and end-all; the Church and 'the "commune" of the realm' merit only passing mention. Even more remarkable is what the letter does *not* say. For the last twelve months English politics had been convulsed by the Charter. Men had been sworn to uphold it and to repudiate it; they had fought for it and against it. But in Louis' letter it is the love that dare not speak its name. There is a highly slanted précis of the *forma securitatis*. But Louis breathes not a word of the Charter itself; much less does he promise to reinstate it.

This is astonishing and too little remarked on. For what are we to deduce from this strange silence? That the baronial leaders like Fitzwalter and de Quincy were no more serious about the Charter than John and that royalist and papal propagandists were right when they denounced the Charter as a mere cloak for baronial ambition? That Fitzwalter and de Quincy were so desperate for French intervention to save their skins that they named no terms? Or was the problem with Louis himself? He had a high Capetian view of kingship. Did this mean that he viewed the Charter with as much disdain as John?

The present state of the evidence offers no simple answers to these questions. But one thing is clear. Louis' failure to commit himself on the Charter left a gaping hole in English politics. It also offered a sweep-the-board opportunity to any politician bold enough to take it.

Once perhaps John, with his reckless gambler's streak of try-anything-once, might have dared to reverse direction yet again. But the king was now a shadow of his former self. His old energy had gone and he sank into a fainéant lassitude. As Louis swept forward from London, John retreated ever further west to Wiltshire and Dorset. Here he lingered for over three weeks at Corfe Castle, one of his favourite residences. John's inactivity gave Louis a free hand

and he laid siege to Winchester. The castle held out for only ten days before John – incomprehensibly – gave the garrison permission to surrender.

The shameful, precipitate surrender of Winchester, which was still the second capital, was a turning point. Confronted with a king who was too cowardly, or too negligent, to defend his own crown, several of the earls who had hitherto remained loyal changed sides. The floor-crossers included John's own bastard half-brother, William Longespee, Earl of Salisbury. Over two-thirds of the baronage had now abandoned John. So too, and still more remarkably, had a third of his household knights, who were the men whose lives, fortunes and loyalties were most closely bound to the king. Even key members of the royal administration were going over and putting their expertise at the service of the invader.

The end seemed near: Louis held the better half of the country with only three castles holding out against him in the south and east – Lincoln, Dover and Windsor – and even they were under siege. There were some signs of patriotic resentment, as the French threw their weight around. But the feeling was neither deep enough nor wide-spread enough to offer a serious threat to Louis' march to the throne.

Then, finally, John roused himself and marched north-east to reinforce his garrison at Lincoln. Perhaps he also hoped to cut off Alexander II of Scotland – whom he hated and despised – on his way home from swearing allegiance to Louis at Canterbury. He missed Alexander but, as consolation, burned and looted the Cambridgeshire countryside as punishment for East Anglia's support for Louis and the barons.

By 9 October he was at Lynn. He dined grossly as usual and suffered a severe attack of dysentery during the night. The attack put him in mortal fear and the following morning he made an expiatory gift to Margaret de Briouze for the souls of her parents and brother. Nevertheless, despite his physical and mental state, he pressed on across the treacherous quicksands of the Wash and reached Swineshead Abbey in Lincolnshire by the evening of the 12th.

The king did but much of his baggage train did not: 'his household effects, his relics and other contents of his chapel' were 'sucked into the quicksand' and lost along with many of their keepers. Eager to keep up with their impetuous king, they had set out in too much of a hurry without waiting for the tide fully to go out.

It was another blow to a dying man. He struggled north for a few more days and arrived at Newark on the 18th. That night he died. Some of his servants pillaged his personal goods and made off with the booty. But enough remained loyal to fulfil his last wishes. He had hoped to be buried at Beaulieu Abbey. But that, like most of his kingdom, was held by his enemies. As second best, he chose Worcester, where his favourite saint, St Wulfstan, had his shrine. There he was buried, near the saint as he wished, and wearing the cowl-like coif which had been placed on his head at his coronation after his anointing with unction.

It was a curiously conventional end for the oddest and strangest of kings.

ELEVEN

NEW KING; NEW CHARTER

Effigy of William Marshal, Earl of Pembroke

John's heir was his nine-year-old son Henry. Henry was an agreeable boy: pious, peace-loving, good-tempered, easily led and neither very bright nor very dim. Normally, in an age where kings had to rule as well as reign, the accession of a minor was difficult at best and disastrous at worst. And the circumstances of 1216 were especially unfavourable. The better half of the country was occupied by a foreign prince and only a rump of the elite remained loyal. The administration had broken down; the treasury was exhausted and the periphery of the country was threatening to break away entirely.

Nevertheless, Henry's accession defied expectations. Far from being a dynastic disaster, it saved the House of Anjou. It also saved the Charter. And it did both thanks largely to one man, William Marshal, Earl of Pembroke.

William Marshal was already seventy and in what should have been the twilight of a long and distinguished career. He was not born great. But he achieved greatness thanks primarily to his prowess as a sportsman. Tall, strong and handsome, with wavy brown hair, he became a star of the international tournament circuit. That also, at a time when the sport of the tournament shaded imperceptibly into real warfare, made him a notable warrior and general. His handiness with sword and lance brought him fame, fortune and a very rich wife. It also gave him the entrée to the Angevin court. Here a different set of qualities came into play as the man's man also turned out to be the consummate courtier. He was deferential to his superiors, affable to his equals and properly considerate (when it suited him) to his inferiors – and all with a shrewd and often ruthless eye to the main chance.

He had need of all this and more to survive and thrive in the entourage of Henry II and his tumultuous family, as father fought with son, husband with wife and brother with brother. But Marshal mostly picked his way through their quarrels with the same dash and dexterity he showed on the battlefield. He misjudged seriously only once when he quarrelled with John in 1205 and spent the next seven years in the political wilderness in self-imposed exile in Ireland on the vast estates he held in right of his wife. But by 1213 all was forgiven.

The turning point came with John's ever more serious dispute with his baronage. Throughout all the ups and downs of his own relationship with the king, Marshal had maintained the ostentatious loyalty that was the chivalric ideal. Perhaps it was a matter of calculation. Perhaps he did it because he believed it. At any rate he now reaped his reward and became the pillar of the regime and the linchpin of the royalist cause. As such, he was John's leading lay negotiator with the barons at The Temple in January 1215, at Oxford in February and at Runnymede itself, where his name appears as the first of 'the noble men' by whose 'advice' (*consilium*) the king had granted Magna Carta.

And yet it seems clear Marshal thought it was all a terrible mistake. This is the only conclusion to be drawn from the treatment of the affair in his remarkable versified biography, *L'Histoire de Guillaume le Maréchal*. The author, who had been commissioned by Marshal's son and was drawing on the recollections of Marshal's friends and contemporaries as well as documents in the family archives, squirms with embarrassment and can barely bring himself to mention what had happened:

> I must pass quickly over the war which broke out between the king and his barons, because there took place too many circumstances which it is not proper to write about. And it could do me harm.

Such was the less than glowing endorsement of the Charter from the circle of the man who would save it.

Marshal had not accompanied John on his last, fatal expedition to Lincolnshire. Instead, he remained in the Marches, where his own principal strength lay, to contain the Welsh and hold the West Country for the king. He seems to have used Gloucester as his main base and it was from there that he set out to meet John's funeral cortège as – in accordance with the king's last wishes – it made its way to Worcester for his obsequies and burial. The embalmed body was escorted by the small group of councillors and intimates, headed by Peter des Roches, Bishop of Winchester, who had remained with John to the end. They bore with them John's written will, the first surviving original testament of an English king, and their stories, true or false, of what he had said on his deathbed.

John's will was a brief, hurried document, only sixteen lines long and heavily abbreviated. The king was already *in extremis* and fading fast: 'hindered by grave infirmity', as he put it when he dictated the will's first sentence. Knowing that he had neither the time nor the capacity to make any detailed provisions – 'not being able at this time of my infirmity to itemise all my things so that I may make a testament' – he committed 'the arbitration and administration of my testament to the trust and to the legitimate administration of my faithful men whose names are written below'. He gave them a few general instructions: to bury him 'in the church of St Mary and St Wulfstan at Worcester'; to make satisfaction to the Church for the injuries he had done; to reward his faithful servants and distribute alms to the poor 'for the salvation of my soul' and to provide 'support to my sons towards obtaining and defending their inheritance'. Otherwise, all was left to the discretion of his 'arbiters and administrators', as men 'without whose counsel, even in good health, I would by no means have arranged my will [save] in their presence'.

Thirteen names follow: those of the churchmen are headed by Cardinal Guala Bicchieri, who had replaced Pandulf as papal legate; and those of the laymen by Marshal.

The open-ended form of the will encouraged speculation about the king's further intentions – then as well as now. The most important witness is Marshal's verse biographer. He gives an accurate list of those who were present at the deathbed; then he reports the king's supposed last words before he was rendered incapable of speech. John, he claims, acknowledged his debt to Marshal, who had always repaid good for ill: 'Always he has served me loyally; never has he acted against me, whatever I have done or said to him.' 'As I am more sure of his loyalty', he continued, 'than that of anybody else, I beg you to entrust him with the guardianship of my son, who will never keep the land, save by him.'

The words have been disputed. But they seem to me to be entirely plausible. Marshal was already the pillar of the old king's regime; what more natural than for him to serve as regent for the new?

He began to act the part immediately. He oversaw the arrangements for John's funeral; then he set in motion Henry's coronation. The boy and his household, who were staying at Devizes, were summoned to Gloucester and

Marshal met them en route at Malmesbury. The boy-king greeted him graciously and entrusted himself to his care: 'God grant you grace to take good care of us', he said. Marshal in turn swore to serve him 'in good faith as long as I have strength'. It was an affecting scene and everyone broke down in tears, 'Marshal like the rest'.

There was some debate about the timing of the coronation. Should they wait for the arrival of the mighty Earl of Chester? Or proceed immediately? They decided to go ahead since 'no one knew what might happen'. So on 28 October – a mere ten days after his father's death – Henry was crowned in a hastily cobbled-together ceremony at Gloucester. His robes were run up to suit his boyish figure and his insignia were make-do-and-mend also since the proper regalia were under enemy control at Westminster.

First Marshal, himself 'the best knight in all the world', gave the boy the accolade and made him 'a pretty little knight'. Then his peers carried him into the cathedral to be made a king. The legate Guala presided and sang mass. But, tactfully, he left the actual business of the coronation to the English bishops who were present. Henry swore the customary coronation oath; performed homage to Guala as the representative of England's new overlord, the pope; and was anointed and crowned with a lady's garland by Peter des Roches, Bishop of Winchester.

The next day, Earl Ranulf of Chester arrived and the lords joined in council to decide the regency. There were only two possible choices: Marshal and Earl Ranulf. Marshal begged to be excused on grounds of his great age. But Ranulf demurred. He listed Marshal's qualities – 'You are so good a knight, so valorous and discreet, so feared, so loved and so wise' – and insisted that only he had the necessary personal prestige.

Guala now took the two candidates aside with a handful of others to settle the matter in private. But it required Guala's offer of absolution from his sins to overcome Marshal's resistance. Finally, the deal was done: Guala absolved him and Marshal undertook the regency as 'guardian (*rector*) of the king and kingdom'.

It was the beginning of a close cooperation between the two men. Innocent III had sent Guala to England in the spring of 1216 to continue his policy of protecting John – as both papal vassal and sworn crusader – with all the armoury of the Faith. Innocent died within a few months of Guala's arrival and John the following October. Nevertheless – despite the new pope, Honorius III, and the new boy-king of England – papal policy continued regardless with Guala as its enthusiastic enforcer. His first act on arriving in England in May 1216 had been to convene a church council at Winchester to excommunicate Louis and his adherents. Now, with his plenary indulgence to Marshal, he was going further and turning the campaign against Louis into a veritable crusade: church and state marched as one, and they marched against the French.

After this period of intense activity, the king, his regent and their little court enjoyed a short break at Tewkesbury Abbey. Then they journeyed south once more to Bristol where the council reconvened. We know nothing of their deliberations. Which is a pity as the decision they arrived at was a momentous one: on 12 November they counselled the boy-king to reissue Magna Carta: 'for God's sake, and for the salvation of our own soul, and of the souls of our ancestors, and of our successors, to the honour of God and the exaltation of Holy Church, and the amendment of our kingdom'.

But it was Magna Carta transformed. First to go, no doubt, was chapter 61. This contained everything that the royalists and the papacy found most objectionable about the Charter: the oath, which put adherence to the charter above loyalty to the king; the clause authorising the 'distraint and distress' of the king, which had sanctioned civil war; and, above all, the Twenty-five with their extraordinary powers of justice and coercion which had been used to reduce John to a doge of Venice and, when he resisted, to declare him dethroned and to elect Louis.

The county juries or commissions of twelve knights, which had been set up by chapter 48 to investigate abuses of the forest laws or misconduct by sheriffs, had produced useful reports which eventually fed into the separate Charter of the Forests. But the open-ended powers of these county commissions meant that they risked turning into local versions of the Twenty-five. So this chapter went too. As did the various chapters requiring the crown to make good 'at once' all the various misdemeanours of John's government. Other chapters were not directly struck out but declared to be 'important yet doubtful' and were parked for further consideration:

> until we have fuller counsel, when we will, most fully in these as well as other matters that have to be amended, do what is for the common good and the peace and estate of ourselves and our kingdom.

What was left was the core of the Charter, which settled feudal incidents (that is the rules governing the transfer of landed property); reformed the administration of justice; standardised weights and measures, and guaranteed the freedom of trade, the free passage of goods and the liberties of cities, towns and ports. These now became law. But they did not fossilise. Indeed, the surprising thing is that, even in the heat and chaos of civil war, the reissued chapters of the Charter contained careful improvements and clarifications.

There remained one final problem: the boy-king had no great seal. Instead, he was made to declare:

> we have had the present charter sealed with the seals of our venerable father, the lord Gualo cardinal priest of St Martin, legate of the apostolic see, and William

Marshal Earl of Pembroke, ruler of us and of our
kingdom.

This made the reversal complete. Guala had been despatched
by the pope who had declared Magna Carta to be 'null and
void of all validity for ever'; Marshal likewise had heartedly
disapproved of the Charter and fought against the men who
had forced it on John 'by violence and fear'. Yet now they
were sanctioning its reissue and giving it, by the application
of their seals, their most formal, public endorsement.

How had this come about? Partly of course it was the
result of expediency and calculation. Louis' failure to
commit himself to the Charter in any way, much less to
reissue it, created an opportunity which his opponents would
have been fools to ignore. And Marshal and Guala were not
fools. But there was conviction as well. Marshal made sure
to send a copy of the reissued Charter to Ireland, which had
remained loyal to John throughout and where the Twenty-
five and their machinations had made no impact whatever.
In other words, Marshal and Guala and the regency council
which they led reissued the Charter because, in its reworked
form, they believed in it and regarded it as a proper basis
on which to reconstruct royal government after the
contrasting excesses of John on the one hand and the
Twenty-five on the other.

The Charter, originally the work of the baronial rebels,
had been adopted by the royalists and adapted to their ends.

At a stroke the Charter, once at the extreme of politics, moved to the centre ground. This guaranteed the future of the Charter. It also set a precedent for the future course of reform in England. Time and again, as in 1215–16, the clothes of the radicals would, after much chewing of fat and occasional spilling of blood, be stolen by the conservatives and, after a modest amount of retailoring, be discovered to fit perfectly.

They would be worn with pride and be proclaimed, after a remarkably short time, to be traditional and quintessentially English. Just like Magna Carta.

TWELVE

VICTORY AND RECONCILIATION

Civil war

The reissuing of Magna Carta on 12 November 1216 was not only tactically shrewd; it also showed the regency council's remarkable confidence in the future of the English monarchy. Whether the confidence was justified was another matter.

A brutal reminder of the real state of affairs had come on the day of the young king's coronation. The service was over; the boy-king had been changed out of his heavy robes into something lighter and the company was about to settle down to the feast when a messenger entered. He addressed Marshal and told him, 'in front of everybody', that his castle of Goodrich was under siege by Louis' party and in desperate need of help. Marshal despatched troops. 'But many who were present thought that this event, on the very day of the coronation, was a bad omen.'

And so it seemed. The prodigious burst of activity of the beginning of Henry III's reign did not last and Marshal found himself presiding over several months of stalemate. As usual, most active campaigning was suspended in the winter. The spring saw an uneasy truce with Louis, who took advantage of it to go back to France to consult and raise more troops. Meanwhile there were the first important defections from the baronial ranks but the hard core of activists remained unshakeably committed to Louis. Louis returned to England in April with 'a numerous and proud army' and, shrugging off the earlier defections, seemed stronger than ever.

At which point the baronial party became careless. They were also bored and restless, having been cooped up in their winter quarters in London. It had been the same two years previously, at the beginning of their armed struggle with John, when they had decided to relieve the tedium of garrison life in London with a tournament at Stamford. Then, wiser counsels had prevailed and the tournament had been moved to the vicinity of the city at Staines. This time, they threw caution to the winds and embarked on what even the sober *Oxford History of England* calls 'a scamper through the midlands'.

The excuse was the fate of Mountsorrel Castle in Leicestershire. The castle, which belonged to Saer de Quincy, Earl of Winchester, was under siege by the royalists. Saer determined to save it; Louis acquiesced and the flower of the baronial party marched north from London. There were over six hundred knights and a thousand foot: the English among them were commanded by Saer and his blood-brother and fellow hard-line rebel, Robert Fitzwalter, and the French by the comte de Perche, marshal of France.

They made a fine sight. But they might have remembered that Marshal was almost always the victor in the tournament.

Hearing of their approach, and knowing their overwhelming strength, the royalist force investing Mountsorrel prudently withdrew to Nottingham before the baronial party even arrived. Balked of a scrap, the barons were all ears for further adventures. One presented itself, temptingly at hand. Mountsorrel lies a few miles to the south of Loughborough; less than fifty miles to the north-east is Lincoln. Nicola de la Hay, the widow of the last castellan, had held its mighty castle for the royalists throughout the barons' wars. A new siege had been levied in the middle of Lent but with no better result than before. The besiegers, hearing of the arrival of the baronial forces, begged for aid. Fitzwalter, de Quincy and the rest were delighted to answer their call. Nottingham and Newark, the principal castles commanding the direct route to Lincoln along the Fosse Way, were in royalist hands. To avoid them, the barons turned east, cutting a swathe through the rich agricultural lands of the Vale of Belvoir, looting and laying waste as they went, before connecting with Ermine Street and marching to Lincoln from the south.

This line of approach brought the baronial forces unchallenged into Lincoln. The medieval town lay on the plain of the River Witham. To the north, and connected to the town by the aptly named Steep Street, was the Roman city of *Lindum*, situated on its high plateau and still with most of its walls intact. The cathedral occupied the south-eastern quadrant of the Roman city; the castle the south-western;

while between the two was an open space now occupied by the besiegers and their baronial reinforcements.

Marshal was at Northampton when he heard news that the baronial flying column had joined the siege of Lincoln. It was the moment he had been waiting for. Louis' forces were divided. And divided they could be destroyed. Marshal covered the eighty-odd miles to Newark in four days of hard riding. But, instead of continuing straight to Lincoln, he made a long detour to the west to the villages of Torkesey and Stow. He was now positioned to approach Lincoln from the north-west, rather than the expected south-west. He also had access to the castle by the western gates, which were not controlled by the besiegers.

Peter des Roches, Bishop of Winchester, who was a warrior-prelate of the old school, took advantage of the circuitous approach to reconnoitre. Accompanied with only a small escort, he got access to the castle to let the garrison know help was at hand; he also discovered a filled-in gate that – unbeknown to the besiegers – led from the castle into the Roman town. Des Roches ordered the gate to be opened up and then returned to the royalist army.

The legate Guala and Marshal addressed the troops. Guala, robed and vested to excommunicate the French and absolve the English, assured them of salvation; Marshal promised them honour. And it worked: 'they were as cheerful as though it had been a question of a tournament'.

Marshal was imbued with the same spirit. Indeed he was

so eager to fight that he rode into battle without his helmet and had to be called back to be armed. But then, over seventy though he was, he performed miracles, using his height and weight and skilled horsemanship to thrust himself three lances deep into the mêlée. The French and their baronial allies, with at least a third more knights than the English, had the advantage of numbers. But, as the English poured through the breech in the walls, the French found themselves taken by surprise in the confined space between the eastern gates of the castle and the west front of the cathedral.

In the general confusion, just as in the contemporary tournament, there were epic personal encounters: Marshal struck one rebel such a blow between his shoulders that he slipped off his horse and fled the field; then Marshal seized the bridle of the French commander, the comte de Perche. Perche, grasping his great sword with both hands, landed three massive strokes on Marshal's helmet, badly denting it. It was the last reflex of a born warrior. Perche reeled in the saddle and fell from his horse. Marshal, thinking that the count, who was his first cousin, had only fainted, ordered his helmet to be removed. At which point, it became clear that he was dead, as a fragment of a sword, which had penetrated his visor, was still protruding from his eye socket.

Their commander slain, the French fell back down Steep Street. Then they rallied and tried to fight their way back up. This was gallant. But it proved fatal as they were caught between Marshal and the main weight of the English bearing down on them from the Roman city and the English rear-guard who had broken into the medieval town and were attacking them from behind. Defeat turned into a rout and over four hundred knights were taken prisoner, including the two diehard baronial leaders, de Quincy and Fitzwalter.

The disaster forced Louis to negotiate. But the talks broke down over the fate of his ecclesiastical supporters, like Simon Langton. Guala wished to inflict severe punishment; Louis was determined to protect them. The French, with Blanche of Castile herself taking the initiative, then made a final effort and put together a fleet to bring in large reinforcements. But the English, with Marshal himself being barely dissuaded from taking to sea, inflicted another major defeat on the French in a naval battle fought off Sandwich, in which the French flagship was boarded, its commander beheaded as a pirate and the troops it was carrying captured and imprisoned.

Louis now had no choice but to take the terms offered him. Marshal, however, made sure they were not too onerous. Louis renounced the throne and promised never to assist English rebels again. On the other hand, his departure was sweetened by a substantial indemnity of 10,000 marks or nearly seven thousand pounds sterling, most of which was paid within the year. Nor were the English rebel barons treated harshly. Quite the contrary. They were given a general amnesty, with restoration of land and freedom from all ransoms.

Indeed the terms were so generous that later Henry III professed to believe that Marshal had betrayed him by not fighting Louis to the finish. But there was wisdom in Marshal's moderation. There was also principle. Marshal had fought the war as a *preux chevalier* – 'a very perfect gentle knight' – not as a royalist ideologue. The rebel barons had been excommunicated; they had *not* been proclaimed traitors. Here I think Marshal was drawing on his own experience when he had spectacularly fallen from grace under John.

John had accused him of treason and, there and then, had demanded that the magnates present at court pass judgment on him. But they refused after Marshal had warned them of what was at stake in agreeing to a charge of treason: 'Be on alert against the king: what he thinks to do to with me, he will do to each and every one of you, or even more, if he gets the upper hand over you.' It is immensely to Marshal's credit that he remained faithful to this position when he himself stood in the king's shoes as regent.

The result was that the wounds of civil war knit up quickly. Indeed they left so few scars that we have forgotten both the magnitude of the issues at stake and the depth of division they engendered. Magna Carta *was* revolutionary; the idea of monarchy *was* shaken to its foundations; the republican challenge *was* real. That it all ended in a classic English compromise was *not* inevitable. And without Marshal it would probably never have happened at all.

It is also important to look at the other side of the picture. The great baronial leaders, Fitzwalter and de Quincy, had been bested. But there was no shame in being beaten in battle by 'the best knight in all the world'. Their power base in the Twenty-five had been destroyed. But the central ideas of Magna Carta were retained in the reissue of the Charter in 1216 and became inviolable.

Honour, that most important of aristocratic values, had been saved all round.

King John. The St Alban's chroniclers present a deeply hostile view of John but here the Abbey workshop shows him as the conventionally pious founder of Beaulieu Abbey.

Philip Augustus (*left*), in the fleurs-de-lys of France, and
John (*right*), in the three lions of England, leading their armies.
Philip won every significant battle between the two.

Philip Augustus (*left*) winning the peace as well as John (*right*), who had lost most of
the Angevin Empire in France, performs homage for his remaining French territories

Henry I's Coronation Charter. The Charter, issued as a sort of manifesto for the throne, served as a model to John's rebellious barons for their attempt to limit royal power.

Innocent III. One of the greatest medieval popes, Innocent had clashed bitterly with John during the Interdict, but, following John's surrender, became his most steadfast protector.

Seal of Stephen Langton, Archbishop of Canterbury. His appointment led to the clash between church and state known as the Interdict but, as archbishop, he strove for neutrality between the king and barons.

The interior of The Temple Church. John often used The Temple, the headquarters of the Knights Templar, as his London base and his first confrontations with his rebellious barons took place here.

The Articles of the Barons, agreed at Runnymede in early June, are a summary draft of Magna Carta, with only the 'security clause' written out in full in the last long paragraph.

The Treaty for the Custody of London (*detail*). John's copy of the 'Indenture' was separated from its counterpart by the wavy cut at the top and sealed by the barons at the bottom.

The two-sided Great Seal of John. This impression was originally attached to the Articles of the Barons (*opposite*); another would have been fixed to the barons' copy of the Treaty (*above*).

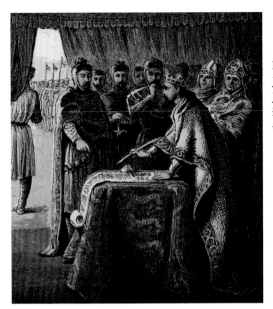

Myths of Magna Carta (1): John signing the Charter. John was probably illiterate; in any case, royal documents were not signed but sealed.

Myths of Magna Carta (2): Magna Carta being sealed at Runnymede. No such 'original' sealed copy of Magna Carta exists; indeed it is impossible that one could have been prepared so quickly.

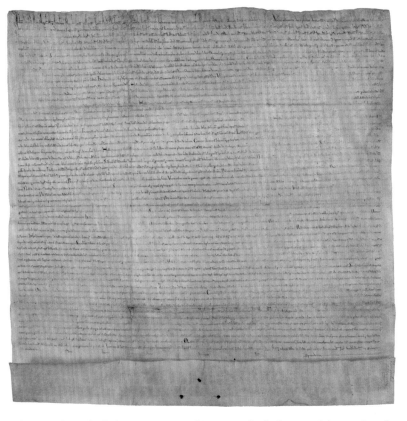

The Lincoln Cathedral Magna Carta. This is one of only four surviving copies of Magna Carta and the only one still in the county to which it was sent in June 1215.

The preparation of parchment. The sheep skin, scraped clean with the semi-circular adze, is stretched to dry in a frame, and the finished, trimmed membrane handed over to a scribe.

A medieval scribe at work. He writes with a quill pen and holds a knife in his left hand. The knife was used to cut the nib and scrape out mistakes from the parchment.

A king dictates the laws to a scribe. Dictation was also used to make enrolments and create multiple copies of documents, like royal writs and Magna Carta itself.

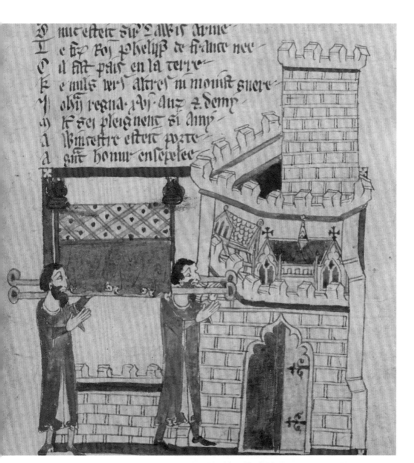

King John's body, in a coffin draped with an elaborate pall, is carried to Worcester for burial in the cathedral.

King John's tomb effigy in Worcester Cathedral. The effigy cannot be treated as a reliable portrait since it was probably made when John's body was transferred to a new sarcophagus in 1232.

Archbishop Langton crowning Henry III in his second coronation in 1220 at Westminster Abbey. This was a magnificent ceremony, in contrast to his first scratch coronation at Gloucester in 1216.

William Marshal, Earl of Pembroke, in combat. Marshal made his name and fortune as the rarely defeated star of the international tournament circuit.

The Durham Cathedral Magna Carta of 1216. Reissued in the name of the young Henry III and sealed with the seals of the papal legate Guala (*left*) and William Marshal (*right*), this heavily edited version saved the Charter.

Prince Louis landing at Sandwich in May 1216. Louis' arrival with a powerful army rescued the baronial cause in England and threatened to depose both John and the Angevin dynasty.

The battle of Lincoln, 1217, showing the castle, flying the English royal standard, the death of the comte de Perche by a sword stroke through the visor, and the defeated French in flight.

The battle of Sandwich, 1217. The defeat of the French and the beheading of their commander as a pirate (*right*) marked the end of Louis's attempt to make himself king of England.

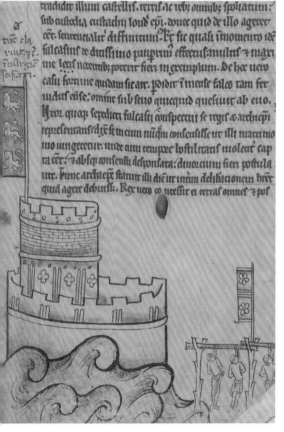

The siege of Bedford Castle, 1224. Sieges were central to the struggle for control in England between 1215 and 1225. But this was the first time a defeated garrison was executed (*right*).

The Magna Carta of 1225. This Charter, reissued in the sole name of Henry III, sealed with his Great Seal and granted in return for taxation, became the definitive version of Magna Cart

THIRTEEN

SPONTANEOUS
AND FREE CONSENT

Excommunication

Despite the achievement of Henry III's regency government, there remained one glaring anomaly: the re-issued Charter of 1216 had been sealed, not with the king's great seal, but with the seals of his 'rectors', Cardinal Guala and William Marshal, Earl of Pembroke. As the king approached his majority, the question became pressing: would he reissue it once more as his own authentic act or not?

The matter greatly exercised the most important survivor of the fraught politics of the original Magna Carta, Stephen Langton. Langton had been allowed to return to England and resume his position as Archbishop of Canterbury in 1219. But he only recovered his full authority when, in 1221 and at the price of another visit to Rome, he obtained the recall of the legate Pandulf. Langton now became the moderating force in a triumvirate of councillors who jockeyed for power under the eighteen-year-old king.

Two years later, in December 1223, the first steps were taken to declaring Henry of age. The following month, at a council held at Westminster, the barons, with Langton acting as their spokesman, called for a confirmation of the Charter. One royal councillor, William Brewer, who had cut his teeth in financial administration under John, argued forcefully against the demand. 'The liberties you demand', he declared, 'since they were extorted by force, ought not by right to be observed.' Back in 1215 Langton, as we have seen, had had similar doubts about the validity of the Charter. But in 1224 he would have no truck with the argument and reproved Brewer sharply. 'William', he remonstrated, 'if you loved the king, you would not [thus] disturb the peace of the kingdom.'

The king now intervened to defuse the situation. 'We have sworn to observe all these liberties', he assured the assembly, 'and what we have sworn we are bound to abide by.' The king's word was better than nothing. But it still fell far short of a formal confirmation.

A fresh opportunity came in 1225. Prince Louis, who succeeded Philip Augustus in 1223 as Louis VIII, took advantage of Henry III's minority to seize the remainder of Poitou. To recover his lands Henry asked for a large grant of taxation of a fifteenth on all moveable property. The king's request was considered at a broadly representative meeting of the council at Westminster at which 'the clergy and people and nobles' were present. 'After some deliberation', the grant was agreed. But on one condition: that the king 'would grant them their long-sought rights'.

Henry and his councillors leapt at the offer and the Charter was reissued, as the council had requested, on 11 February 1225. Its text followed closely that of 1216 – but with a few, crucial differences. The first came in the preamble, when the words *spontanea et bona voluntate nostra*, 'spontaneously and of our own free will', were inserted. At a stroke, the taint of coercion, which had vitiated Magna Carta, and still polluted the Charters in the long memory of William Brewer in 1223, was removed.

Another, little noted step further emphasised the king's sole agency in reissuing the Charter. In both 1215 and 1216 the king was declared to have issued the Charter 'by the advice' of his clerical and lay councillors, who are then listed by name in order of precedence. In 1225, however, there is no mention of advice and no listing of councillors. Instead the king grants alone, *mero motu* 'of his own mere motion and desire', as the usual formula in royal letters patent recites. And the magnates, far from participating in his action as councillors, merely testify to it as witnesses to the Charter – and to its sealing with the king's own great seal.

Henry had been given a great seal in 1218, but only on condition that, for the duration of his minority, it could not be used to authenticate grants in perpetuity. In December 1223 Langton connived in giving the king nominal control over the seal. And, just over a year later in 1225, he participated in the fudge which allowed Henry, though still two years under age, to reissue the Charter of liberties *in perpetuum*, 'for ever'.

It almost looks as though Langton had planned the outcome all along.

The list of witnesses is also testimony to the work of William Marshal, who had died in 1219, in reconciling and knitting up division. Three of the lay magnates (the earls of Salisbury and Warenne and Hubert de Burgh) had been among King John's advisers at Runnymede; while no fewer than six (Robert Fitzwalter, Gilbert de Clare, Hugh Bigod, Robert de Ros, Richard de Mountfichet, and William d'Aubigny) had been among his bitterest opponents as members of the Twenty-five. Even William Brewer, despite his vehemently expressed reservations only two years earlier in 1223, was present to witness and endorse the reissue.

Even more far-reaching was the final, and entirely new, clause which explained the circumstances of the reissue. This was frank in presenting the Charter as a direct *quid pro quo* or bargain:

> And for this our grant and gift of these liberties . . . the archbishops, bishops, abbots, priors, earls, barons, knights, freeholders, and all of our realm have given us a fifteenth part of all their moveables.

A last sentence was borrowed from the contentious chapter 61 of 1215:

> We have also granted to them for us and our heirs that neither we nor our heirs will procure anything whereby

the liberties contained in this charter shall be infringed or weakened; and if any thing contrary to this is procured from anyone, it shall avail nothing and be held for nought.

In 1215, this clause had been intended – unsuccessfully, of course – to prevent John from appealing to Rome against the Charter. It reappeared, rather anomalously, in 1225 to guard against the fact that this reissue, unlike 1215 or 1216, lacked the endorsement of a papal legate.

But if Rome had not directly endorsed the Charter, the English church, as embodied in its forceful primate, Stephen Langton, did. The 1225 Charter, with the removal of the taint of coercion, satisfied him morally. It also, with its invocation of a broadly inclusive 'community of realm' – which embraced 'everybody in our kingdom', from archbishops and magnates to the humblest free man – corresponded to his vision of a Christian polity: all of them had paid the fifteenth on the one hand and all of them were the beneficiaries of the Charter on the other.

It really was a case of 'we are all in this together'. And the Church, so reluctant, divided and ambiguous in 1215, was henceforward to the fore in the defence and propagation of the Charter. Soon after the reissue of 1225, Langton led his suffragans in proclaiming a sentence of excommunication on all who should violate the Charter. In 1227 he obtained permission for his brother, Simon, the most passionate and articulate ideologue of the baronial movement of 1215, to return from a decade of exile. And in January 1228, almost certainly at Langton's initiative, Pope Gregory IX, as both supreme pontiff and feudal overlord, finally gave formal confirmation of the Charter.

A few months later, in July 1228, Langton died, aged almost eighty and vigorous in mind to the last. He was a notable scholar and both a defender and reformer of the Church. But his greatest achievement was to tie church and Magna Carta together: 'to have started a tradition of the use of Magna Carta by English bishops as a symbol of limited monarchy (not merely of the freedom of the church)'.

And, following in his footsteps, Langton's successors repeated the sentence of excommunication against violators of the Charter on its next reissue in 1237 and again in 1253. This last was an occasion of high ceremony. It took place in Westminster Hall on 12 May 1253 when, in the king's own presence, the Archbishop of Canterbury and thirteen other bishops pronounced the solemn sentence with candles burning and bells ringing.

They invoked the Trinity, the Virgin Mary, Saints Peter and Paul, all saints and martyrs and, in particular, St Thomas Becket, who had been martyred in defence of the freedom of the English church, and Edward the Confessor, whose laws were supposed to be the foundation of Magna Carta. They then proceeded to 'excommunicate, anathematise and sequester from the threshold of Holy Mother Church' all who deprived churches of their rights. Or who violated, infringed or diminished the free customs and liberties of the realm, especially those contained in the Charter. Or who broke the peace of the realm.

The sentence pronounced, the candles were cast down and, as they were still smouldering on the ground, everyone said in unison: 'Thus are extinguished and stink in hell those who attack this sentence.' Bells were rung and the king himself declared: 'So help me God, I will faithfully guard all these terms inviolate, as I am a man, as I am a Christian, as I am a knight, and as I am a crowned and anointed king.' Henry had been offered a lighted candle to hold with the bishops as they proclaimed the sentence. But he declined it as improper because he was not an ordained priest. Instead – like an American president – 'he held his hand to his chest for the entirety of the sentence, with a cheerful expression on his face'.

In less than half a century and within the lifetime of a single king, Magna Carta had metamorphosed from a revolutionary and incendiary tract into a solemn text, sanctified and honoured and paraded in the theatre of royal and ecclesiastical ceremony.

It was not an outcome that anyone in 1215 could have foreseen. Apart perhaps from Stephen Langton.

FOURTEEN

AFTER MAGNA CARTA:
A TALE OF TWO CHARTERS

*'The Revolution Seal', detail from the
State Seal Window in the Massachusetts State House, Boston*

The events of 1215 were a revolution. The baronial leaders were violent, radical and aimed at the overthrow of royal government. Magna Carta was both their manifesto and their instrument. If John had accepted the Charter, the powers of the Twenty-five would have turned him into a doge of Venice and England into an aristocratic republic. When he resisted, the baronial leaders went further and envisaged — however temporarily — a world without kings and a realm ruled by overtly republican forms.

This of course is not the Magna Carta that is being presented to us in this, its 800th anniversary year. This Magna Carta is safe, domesticated, comforting. But it *is* the Magna Carta of the earliest contemporary account in the chronicle of Melrose Abbey:

> a new state of things [has] begun in England; such a
> strange affair as had never before been heard; for the
> body wished to rule the head, and the people desired
> to be masters over the king.

The language is apocalyptic because the writer or his informant had seen 'a new heaven and a new earth' — or at least a new Jerusalem being built at Runnymede in England's green and pleasant land.

But of course the revolution failed; the republic died and the walls of the new Jerusalem crumbled and turned to dust. Magna Carta should have been forgotten with the rest. That it was not was due to very different circumstances and men of a very different stamp also.

Chief among them was William Marshal, Earl of Pembroke. It was he who, as regent for the young Henry III, took the decision to reissue the Charter within a few weeks of John's death. Marshal was centrist, courtier-like and conventional. He was the ultimate conservative: loyal, royalist and without a trace of radicalism. The reissued Charter reflected its author. Not only was chapter 61, which set up the revolutionary machinery of the Twenty-five, struck out in its entirety, so too were numerous other chapters that were deemed to be 'important yet doubtful'. In Marshal's world there was no room for 'doubtful' or difficult ideas, let alone dangerous ones.

This is not a temperament that is much regarded nowadays – even in political parties that affect to call themselves conservative. And yet it was Marshal who saved the Charter. He did so principally for straightforward reasons of expediency. His young charge was in desperate need of all the support that he could get and the reissued Charter, shorn of its most contentious chapters, was an obvious device to win over the waverers and the undecided to the cause of Henry III.

This is not at all idealistic. It is not very lofty. But it is not reprehensible either. Must men always act idealistically or selflessly? Is there not something to be said for those who come up with a practical solution to a practical problem? Marshal's reissue of the Charter was just that.

Nor, by the way, was it hypocritical. Marshal sent a copy of the reissued Charter to Ireland, where the lords had remained loyal and there was nothing to be gained by it. So he must have believed its gist was right. He had not been prepared to die in the ditch for it. And he certainly thought it was wrong to overthrow royal government to bring it about. But if it could be introduced calmly and without too much fuss, then well and good.

This, it seems to me, is a properly conservative attitude to reform. And it also passed another properly conservative test: it worked. The reissued Charter played a crucial part in safeguarding the throne of the young Henry III and in ensuring the survival of the Angevin dynasty itself. It became the prototype for the broader pattern of reform in England and it placed Magna Carta at the centre of that process of negotiation and careful compromise.

But *which* Magna Carta? For, as we can now see, there are two. They are separated by only a year and they share much of their text in common. But they are fundamentally different documents. The Magna Carta of 1215 is radical and a product of revolution. The Magna Carta of 1216 is centrist and is the painstaking work of the political process. The former is abortive; the latter is the foundation of English political history.

Which you prefer depends on your temperament and your politics. And different groups have drawn on the one or the other. Generally, of course, the romance and revolutionary fervour of 1215 have proved much the more attractive. Black and white and right and wrong is always a better story than the muddled greys of compromise, negotiation and the middle way.

But, despite the dash and danger, revolution in England has invariably failed while the political process has triumphed.

Till now.

But it is easy to become complacent, as we are doing conspicuously in this 800th anniversary year. We live in easy times and have forgotten what happens when things go wrong. We are bored and we crave excitement. We are ignorant of history and have a child-like belief in the future. Politics and politicians are held in contempt and the necessary mixture of motives and give and take of the political process is despised. The state is expensive, burdensome and intrusive. The law is straining to adapt to new attitudes and technologies. The periphery of Britain is in revolt;

malcontents abound in the elite; our relations with the Continent are fraught; religious radicalism is on the rise.

Is it silly to think there is a touch of 1215? A whiff of revolution in the air? If so, we can only hope that, in the fullness of time, we find a new William Marshal.

On the other side of the Atlantic, however, it all looks very different. Magna Carta is celebrated there too. But so of course is revolution. Revolution in America is not abortive as in England. Nor is a republic a might-have-been. Moreover, both the Revolution and the Republic are seen – once again – as having their foundations in Magna Carta. The text of Magna Carta is incorporated *in extenso* into the constitutions of seventeen of the fifty States; a copy of the Charter is displayed alongside the Declaration of Independence, the Constitution and the Bill of Rights in the Great Hall of the Archives in Washington and another in the basement of the Rotunda of the Capital; while the granting of the Charter is represented in relief on the bronze doors of the Supreme Court, whose Justices have cited the Charter itself over four hundred times in their judgments.

In short, the Charter *lives* in America. Or at least it has acquired a new lease of life.

But it is also a *different* life. In America, the barons have won; chapter 61 – the *forma securitatis* – is not a short-term, misconceived expedient but a far-sighted anticipation of both the letter and the spirit of the federal constitution, with its obsessive distrust of government – *all* government – and its elevation of law into the ruling power of the state.

Indeed, the idea of law itself as *sovereign* is the key. Another bronze relief on the doors of the Supreme Court represents Sir Edward Coke confronting the Stuart King James I. Coke was the leading jurist of early seventeenth-century England and the author of a bold attempt to make Magna Carta fundamental law inviolable by either king or parliament. The attempt failed in England. But it succeeded in America where the Founding Fathers entrenched the Constitution as untouchable, fundamental law, to be interpreted not by Congress, still less by the President, but by the Justices of the Supreme Court.

There, on that side of the Atlantic, the law really is supreme. And if there is a final, sovereign arbiter it is, as Sir Edward Coke would have wished, the judges of the Supreme Court.

So far, England and America appear, as in a parallel case, to be two countries divided by a common Charter. Actually, the similarities are far stronger. In England, as Walter Bagehot pointed out in the high noon of Victoria's reign, 'a Republic has insinuated itself beneath the folds of a Monarchy'. Conversely, in America an imperial presidency wears the diadem ever more blatantly in another sort of crowned republic. There are even recognisable royal families;

almost an order of succession. But, most of all, it is history which unites us and separates the United States from every other contemporary republic. For only the American republic has its roots, not only in a revolution, but in an antecedent history.

In our history. In Magna Carta.

It is this, as well as the astonishingly durable institutional architecture of the eighteenth-century constitutional settlement, which has given the Republic its unique stability. But it also means that, on the new side of the Atlantic as well as the old, there is a certain political lassitude, a weariness of men as well as parties and institutions.

For eight hundred years is a long time for a political culture to survive, thrive and constantly renew itself. Other political systems have lasted longer. But they have done so at the price of fossilisation.

Instead, the men of 1215 sowed a seed, which is a living, growing thing. We must hope that the last of its fruit is not yet harvested.

APPENDIX: THE CHARTERS

APPENDIX. THE CHAPTERS

This book tells the story of how Magna Carta evolved from the revolutionary document of 1215, through the radical revision of 1216, to the constitution-in-the-making of 1225. Here we print the parallel texts of the three Charters; highlight the successive changes and enable the reader to follow the process of revision for themselves.

Magna Carta 1215

John, by the grace of God, king of England, lord of Ireland, duke of Normandy and Aquitaine, and court of Anjou, to the archbishops, bishops, abbots, earls, barons, justiciars, foresters, sheriffs, stewards, servants, and to all his bailiffs and faithful subjects, greeting.

Know that we, out of reverence for God and for the salvation of our soul and those of all our ancestors and heirs, for the honour of God and the exaltation of holy church, and for the reform of our realm, on the advice of[1] our venerable fathers, Stephen, archbishop of Canterbury, primate of all England and cardinal of the holy Roman church, Henry archbishop of Dublin, William of London, Peter of Winchester, Jocelyn of Bath and Glastonbury, Hugh of

Magna Carta 1216

Henry, by the grace of God king of England, lord of Ireland, duke of Normandy and Aquitaine, and count of Anjou, to the archbishops, bishops, abbots, earls, barons, justiciars, foresters, sheriffs, stewards, servants, bailiffs and to all his faithful subjects, greeting.

Know that we, out of reverence for God and for the salvation of our soul and those of all our ancestors and successors, for the honour of God and the exaltation of holy church, and for the reform of our realm, on the advice of[1] our venerable fathers, the lord Gualo, cardinal priest of St Martin, legate of the apostolic see, Peter of Winchester, R. of St Asaph, J. of Bath and Glastonbury, S. of Exeter, R. of Chichester, W. of Coventry, B. of Rochester, H. of Llandaff, –

Magna Carta 1225

Henry by the grace of God, king of England, lord of Ireland, duke of Normandy, Aquitaine, and count of Anjou, to the archbishops, bishops, abbots, priors, earls, barons, sheriffs, stewards, servants and to all his bailiffs and faithful subjects who shall look at the present charter, greeting.

Know that we, out of reverence for God and for the salvation of our soul and the souls of our ancestors and successors, for the exaltation of holy church and the reform of our realm, *have of our own spontaneous goodwill*[2] given and granted to the archbishops, bishops, abbots, priors, earls, barons and *all of our*[3] realm these liberties written below to be held in our kingdom of England for ever,

Notes

1. *The statement, common to both MC 1216 and MC 1216, that the Charter had been issued 'on the advice of' the royal councillors, and the list of their names, is omitted from MC 1225 to emphasise that the Charter is issued purely of the king's free will.*

2. *This new phrase further emphasises that MC 1225 is granted of the king's free will and removes the taint of coercion that had dogged MC hitherto.*

3. *These words enormously broaden the scope of the Charter, from 'all free men' (the minority), to 'all' free and unfree (the great majority) alike.*

Magna Carta 1215 cont'd	Magna Carta 1216 cont'd
Lincoln, Walter of Worcester, William of Coventry and Benedict of Rochester, bishops, of master Pandulf, subdeacon and member of the household of the lord pope, of brother Aymeric, master of the order of Knights Templar in England, and of the noble men William Marshal earl of Pembroke, William earl of Salisbury, William earl of Warenne, William earl of Arundel, Alan of Galloway constable of Scotland, Warin fitz Gerold, Peter fitz Herbert, Hubert de Burgh seneschal of Poitou, Hugh de Neville, Matthew fitz Herbert, Thomas Basset, Alan Basset, Philip de Aubeney, Robert of Ropsley, John Marshal, John fitz Hugh, and others, our faithful subjects:	of St David's, – of Bangor and S. of Worcester, bishops, and of the noble men William Marshal earl of Pembroke, Ranulf earl of Chester, William de Ferrers earl of Derby, William count of Aumale, Hubert de Burgh our justiciar, Savari de Mauléon, William Brewer the father, William Brewer the son, Robert de Courtenay, Fawkes de Breauté, Reynold de Vautort, Walter de Lacy, Hugh de Mortimer, John of Monmouth, Walter de Beauchamp, Walter de Clifford, Roger de Clifford, Robert de Mortimer, William de Cantilupe, Matthew fitz Herbert, John Marshal, Alan Basset, Philip de Aubeney, John Lestrange and others, our faithful subjects:
Chapter 1 (A)	*Chapter 1 (A)*
In the first place have granted to God, and by this our	In the first place have granted to God, and by this our

Magna Carta 1225 cont'd | Notes cont'd

Chapter 1 (A)

In the first place we have
granted to God, and by this

Magna Carta 1215 cont'd	Magna Carta 1216 cont'd
present charter confirmed for us and our heirs for ever that the English church shall be free, and shall have its rights undiminished and its liberties unimpaired; and it is our will that it be thus observed; which is evident from the fact that, before the quarrel between us and our barons began, we willingly and spontaneously granted and by our charter confirmed the freedom of elections[4] which is reckoned most important and very essential to the English church, and obtained confirmation of it from the lord pope Innocent III; the which we will observe and we wish our heirs to observe it in good faith for ever.	present charter confirmed for us and our heirs for ever, that the English church shall be free, and shall have its rights undiminished and its liberties unimpaired.

Chapter 1 (B)	*Chapter 1 (B)*
We have also granted to all free men of our kingdom, for ourselves and our heirs for	We have also granted to all free men of our kingdom, for ourselves and our heirs for

Magna Carta 1225 cont'd

Notes cont'd

our present charter confirmed
for us and our heirs for ever,
that the English church shall
be free and shall have all its
rights undiminished and its
liberties unimpaired.

*4. The guarantee of freedom of
elections, granted by John to the
church in 1214, is omitted from MC
1216 and all subsequent versions of
the Charter.*

Chapter 1 (B)

We have also granted to all
free men of our kingdom, for
ourselves and our heirs for

Magna Carta 1215 cont'd	Magna Carta 1216 cont'd
ever, all the liberties written below, to be had and held by them and their heirs of us and our heirs.	ever, all the liberties written below, to be had and held by them and their heirs for ever, all the liberties written below, to be had and held by them and their heirs of us and our heirs.

Chapter 2

Chapter 2

If any of our earls or barons or others holding of us in chief by knight service dies, and at his death his heir be of full age and owe relief he shall have his inheritance on payment of the old relief, namely the heir or heirs of an earl; £100 for a whole earl's barony, the heir or heirs of a baron £100 for a whole barony, the heir or heirs of a knight 100s, at most, for a whole knight's fee; and he who owes less shall give less according to the ancient usage of fiefs.	If any of our earls or barons or others holding of us in chief by knight service dies, and at his death his heir be of full age and owe relief he shall have his inheritance on payment of the old relief, namely the heir or heirs of an earl £100 for a whole earl's barony, the heir or heirs of a baron £100 for a whole barony, the heir or heirs of a knight 100s, at most, for a whole knight's fee; and he who owes less shall give less according to the ancient usage of fiefs.

Magna Carta 1225 cont'd | Notes cont'd

ever, all the liberties written below to be had and held by them and their heirs of us and our heirs for ever.

Chapter 2

If any of our earls or barons or others holding of us in chief by knight service dies, and at his death his heir be of full age and owe relief he shall have his inheritance on payment of the old relief, namely the heir or heirs of an earl £100 for a whole earl's barony, the heir or heirs of a baron £100 for a whole barony, the heir or heirs of a knight 100s, at most, for a whole knight's fee; and he who owes less shall give less according to the ancient usage of fiefs.

Magna Carta 1215 cont'd	Magna Carta 1216 cont'd
Chapter 3[5]	*Chapter 3*[5]
If, however, the heir of any such be under age and a ward, he shall have his inheritance when he comes of age without paying relief and without making fine.	If, however, the heir of any such be under age, his lord shall not have wardship of him, nor of his land, before he has received his homage; and after being a ward such an heir shall have his inheritance when he comes of age, that is of twenty-one years, without paying relief and without making fine, so, however, that if he is made a knight while still under age, the land nevertheless shall remain in his lord's wardship for the full term.
Chapter 4	*Chapter 4*
The guardian of the land of such an heir who is under age shall take from the land of the heir no more than reasonable revenues, reasonable customary dues and reasonable services, and that without destruction and waste of men	The guardian of the land of such an heir who is under age shall take from the land of the heir no more than reasonable revenues, reasonable customary dues and reasonable services, and that without destruction and waste of men

Magna Carta 1225 cont'd	Notes cont'd
Chapter 3	5. *The two versions of Chapter 3 show that, even in the difficult circumstances of a new reign, a royal minority and civil war, careful thought was being given to improving and elaborating the provisions of the Charter.*
If, however, the heir of any such be under age, his lord shall not have wardship of him, nor of his land, before he has received his homage; and after being a ward such an heir shall have his inheritance when he comes of age, that is of twenty-one years, without paying relief and without making fine, so, however, that if he is made a knight while still under age, the land nevertheless shall remain in the wardship of his lords for the full term.	
Chapter 4	
The guardian of the land of such an heir who is under age shall take from the land of the heir no more than reasonable revenues, reasonable customary dues and reasonable services, and that without destruction and waste of men or goods;	

Magna Carta 1215 cont'd

or goods; and if we commit the wardship of the land of any such to a sheriff, or to any other who is answerable to us for its revenues, and he destroys or wastes what he has wardship of, we will take compensation from him and the land shall be committed to two lawful and discreet men of that fief, who shall be answerable for the revenues to us or to him to whom we have assigned them; and if we give or sell to anyone the wardship of any such land and he causes destruction or waste therein, he shall lose that wardship, and it shall be transferred to two lawful and discreet men of that fief who shall similarly be answerable to us as is aforesaid.

Chapter 5

Moreover, so long as he has the wardship of the land, the

Magna Carta 1216 cont'd

or goods; and if we commit the wardship of the land of any such to a sheriff, or to any other who is answerable to us for the revenues of that land, and he destroys or wastes what he has wardship of, we will take compensation from him and the land shall be committed to two lawful and discreet men of that fief, who shall be answerable for the revenues to us or to him to whom we have assigned them; and if we give or sell to anyone the wardship of any such land and he causes destruction or waste therein, he shall lose that wardship and it shall be transferred to two lawful and discreet men of that fief, who shall similarly be answerable to us as is aforesaid.

Chapter 5

Moreover, so long as he has the wardship of the land, the

Magna Carta 1225 cont'd | Notes cont'd

and if we commit the wardship of the land of any such to a sheriff, or to any other who is answerable to us for the revenues of that land, and he destroys or wastes what he has wardship of, we will take compensation from him and the land shall be committed to two lawful and discreet men of that fief, who shall be answerable for the revenues to us or to him to whom we have assigned them; and if we give or sell to anyone the wardship of any such land and he causes destruction or waste therein, he shall lose that wardship and it shall be transferred to two lawful and discreet men of that fief, who shall similarly be answerable to us as is aforesaid.

Chapter 5

Moreover, so long as he has the wardship of the land, the

Magna Carta 1215 cont'd	Magna Carta 1216 cont'd
guardian shall keep in repair the houses, parks, preserves, ponds, mills, and other things pertaining to the land out of the revenues from it; and he shall restore to the heir when he comes of age his land fully stocked with ploughs and the means of husbandry according to what the season of husbandry requires and the revenues of the land can reasonably bear.	guardian shall keep in repair the houses, parks, preserves, ponds, mills and other things pertaining to the land out of the revenues from it; and he shall restore to the heir when he comes of age his land fully stocked with ploughs and all other things in at least the measure he received. All these things shall be observed in the case of wardships of vacant archbishoprics, bishoprics, abbeys, priories, churches and dignities except that wardships of this kind may not be sold.
Chapter 6	*Chapter 6*
Heirs shall be married without disparagement, yet so that before the marriage is contracted those nearest in blood to the heir shall have notice.	Heirs shall be married without disparagement.

172

Magna Carta 1225 cont'd

guardian shall keep in repair
the houses, parks, preserves,
ponds, mills and other things
pertaining to the land out of
the revenues from it; and he
shall restore to the heir when
he comes of age his land fully
stocked with ploughs and all
other things in at least the
measure he received. All these
things shall be observed in the
case of wardships of vacant
archbishoprics, bishoprics,
abbeys, priories, churches and
dignities that pertain to us
except that wardships of this
kind may not be sold.

Chapter 6

Heirs shall be married without
disparagement.

Magna Carta 1215 cont'd	Magna Carta 1216 cont'd
Chapter 7	*Chapter 7*
A widow shall have her marriage portion and inheritance forthwith and without difficulty after the death of her husband; nor shall she pay anything to have her dower or her marriage portion or the inheritance which she and her husband held on the day of her husband's death; and she may remain in her husband's house for forty days after his death, within which time her dower will be assigned to her.	A widow shall have her marriage portion and inheritance forthwith and without any difficulty after the death of her husband; nor shall she pay anything to have her dower or her marriage portion or the inheritance which she and her husband held on the day of her husband's death; and she may remain in her husband's house for forty days after his death, within which time her dower shall be assigned to her, unless it has already been assigned to her or unless the house is a castle; and if she leaves the castle, a suitable house shall be immediately provided for her in which she can stay honourably until her dower is assigned to her in accordance with what is aforesaid.

Magna Carta 1225 cont'd	Notes cont'd

Chapter 7

A widow shall have her
marriage portion and inheritance forthwith and without
any difficulty after the death
of her husband, nor shall she
pay anything to have her
dower or her marriage portion
or the inheritance which she
and her husband held on the
day of her husband's death;
and she may remain in the
chief house of her husband for
forty days after his death,
within which time her dower
shall be assigned to her, unless
it has already been assigned to
her or unless the house is a
castle; and if she leaves the
castle, a suitable house shall be
immediately provided for her
in which she can stay honour-
ably until her dower is
assigned to her in accordance
with what is aforesaid, and she
shall have meanwhile her
reasonable estover of common.
There shall be assigned to her

Magna Carta 1215 cont'd	Magna Carta 1216 cont'd
Chapter 8	*Chapter 8*
No widow shall be forced to marry so long as she wishes to live without a husband, provided that she gives security not to marry without our consent if she holds of us, or without the consent of her lord of whom she holds, if she holds of another.	No widow shall be forced to marry so long as she wishes to live without a husband, provided that she gives security not to marry without our consent if she holds of us, or without the consent of her lord if she holds of another.
Chapter 9	*Chapter 9*
Neither we nor our bailiffs will seize for any debt any land or rent, so long as the chattels of the debtor are sufficient to repay the debt; nor will those who have gone surety for the debtor be distrained so long as the	We or our bailiffs will not seize for any debt any land or rent, so long as the available chattels of the debtor are sufficient to repay the debt and the debtor himself is prepared to have it paid therefrom; nor will those who have gone

Magna Carta 1225 cont'd	Notes cont'd

for her dower a third of all
her husband's land which was
his in his lifetime, unless a
smaller share was given her at
the church door.

Chapter 8

No widow shall be forced to
marry so long as she wishes to
live without a husband,
provided that she gives security not to marry without our
consent if she holds of us, or
without the consent of her
lord if she holds of another.

Chapter 9

We or our bailiffs will not
seize for any debt any land or
rent, so long as the available
chattels of the debtor are sufficient to repay the debt and the
debtor himself is prepared to
have it paid therefrom; nor
will those who have gone

Magna Carta 1215 cont'd

Magna Carta 1216 cont'd

principal debtor is himself able
to pay the debt; and if the
principal debtor fails to pay
the debt having nothing
where-with to pay it, then
shall the sureties answer for
the debt; and they shall, if
they wish, have the lands and
rents of the debtor until they
are reimbursed for the debt
which they have paid for him,
unless the principal debtor can
show that he has discharged
his obligation in the matter to
the said sureties.

surety for the debtor be
distrained so long as the principal debtor is himself able to
pay the debt; and if the principal debtor fails to pay the
debt, having nothing where-
with to pay it or is able but
unwilling to pay, then shall the
sureties answer for the debt;
and they shall, if they wish,
have the lands and rents of the
debtor until they are reimbursed for the debt which they
have paid for him, unless the
principal debtor can show that
he has discharged his
obligation in the matter to the
said sureties.

Chapter 10[6]

If anyone who has borrowed
from the Jews any sum, great
or small, dies before it is
repaid, the debt shall not bear
interest as long as the heir is
under age, of whomsoever he
holds; and if the debt falls into

Magna Carta 1225 cont'd

surety for the debtor be distrained so long as the principal debtor is himself able to pay the debt; and if the principal debtor fails to pay the debt, having nothing wherewith to pay it or is able but unwilling to pay, then shall the sureties answer for the debt; and they shall, if they wish, have the lands and rents of the debtor until they are reimbursed for the debt which they have paid for him, unless the principal debtor can show that he has discharged his obligation in the matter to the said sureties.

Notes cont'd

6. *This chapter, 'on debts of Jews and others', was one of those deemed to be 'important yet doubtful', and dropped from MC 1216 and all subsequent versions of the Charter (see MC 1216 Chapter 42 below).*

Magna Carta 1215 cont'd	Magna Carta 1216 cont'd
our hands, we will not take anything except the principal mentioned in the bond.	

Chapter 11[7]

And if anyone dies indebted to the Jews, his wife shall have her dower and pay nothing of that debt; and if the dead man leaves children who are under age, they shall be provided with necessaries befitting the holding of the deceased; and the debt shall be paid out of the residue, reserving, however, service due to lords of the land, debts owing to others than Jews shall be dealt with in like manner.

Chapter 12[8]

No scutage or aid shall be imposed in our kingdom unless by common counsel of our kingdom, except for ransoming our person, for

Magna Carta 1225 cont'd	Notes cont'd
	7. This chapter, 'on debts of Jews and others', was one of those deemed to be 'important yet doubtful', and dropped from MC 1216 and all subsequent versions of the Charter (see MC 1216 Chapter 42 below).
	8. This chapter, 'on the assessing of scutage and aids', was one of those deemed to be 'important yet doubtful', and dropped from MC 1216 and all subsequent versions of the Charter (see MC 1216 Chapter 42 below).

Magna Carta 1215 cont'd	Magna Carta 1216 cont'd
making our eldest son a knight, and for once marrying our eldest daughter; and for these only a reasonable aid shall be levied. Be it done in like manner concerning aids from the city of London.	

Chapter 13	*Chapter 10*
And the city of London shall have all its ancient liberties and free customs as well by land as by water. Furthermore, we will and grant that all other cities, boroughs, towns, and ports shall have all their liberties and free customs.	The city of London shall have all its ancient liberties and free customs. Furthermore, we will and grant that all other cities, boroughs, towns, the barons of the Cinque Ports, and all ports shall have all their liberties and free customs.

Chapter 14[9]

And to obtain the common counsel of the kingdom about the assessing of an aid (except in the three cases aforesaid) or of a scutage, we will cause to be summoned the archbishops, bishops, abbots, earls and greater

Magna Carta 1225 cont'd	Notes cont'd

Chapter 10

The city of London shall have all its ancient liberties and free customs. Furthermore, we will and grant that all other cities, boroughs, towns, the barons of the Cinque Ports, and all ports shall have all their liberties and free customs.

9. This chapter, 'on the assessing of scutage and aids', was one of those deemed to be 'important yet doubtful', and dropped from MC 1216 and all subsequent versions of the Charter (see MC 1216 Chapter 42 below).

Magna Carta 1215 cont'd | Magna Carta 1216 cont'd

barons, individually by our
letters – and, in addition, we will
cause to be summoned generally
through our sheriffs and bailiffs
all those holding of us in chief –
for a fixed date, namely, after the
expiry of at least forty days, and
to a fixed place; and in all letters
of such summons we will specify
the reason for the summons.
And when the summons has
thus been made, the business
shall proceed on the day
appointed, according to the
counsel of those present,
though not all have come who
were summoned.

Chapter 15[10]

We will not in future grant any
one the right to take an aid from
his free men, except for
ransoming his person, for
making his eldest son a knight
and for once marrying his eldest
daughter, and for these only a
reasonable aid shall be levied.

Magna Carta 1225 cont'd	Notes cont'd
	10. This chapter, 'on the assessing of scutage and aids', was one of those deemed to be 'important yet doubtful', and dropped from MC 1216 and all subsequent versions of the Charter (see MC 1216 Chapter 42 below).

Magna Carta 1215 cont'd	Magna Carta 1216 cont'd
Chapter 16	*Chapter 11*
No one shall be compelled to do greater service for a knight's fee or for any other free holding than is due from it.	No one shall be compelled to do greater service for a knight's fee or for any other free holding than is due from it.
Chapter 17	*Chapter 12*
Common pleas shall not follow our court, but shall be held in some fixed place.	Common pleas shall not follow our court, but shall be held in some fixed place.
Chapter 18	*Chapter 13*
Recognitions of novel disseisin, of mort d'ancester, and of darrein presentment, shall not be held elsewhere than in the counties to which they relate, and in this manner – we, or, if we should be out of the realm, our chief justiciar, will send two justices through each county four times a year, who, with four knights of each county chosen by the county, shall hold the said assizes in the county and	Recognitions of novel disseisin, of mort d'ancestor, and of darrein presentment, shall not be held elsewhere than in the counties to which they relate, and in this manner – we, or, if we should be out of the realm, our chief justiciar, will send two justices through each county four times a year, who, with four knights of each county chosen by the county, shall hold the said assizes in the county and

Magna Carta 1225 cont'd	Notes cont'd
Chapter 11 No one shall be compelled to do greater service for a knight's fee or for any other free holding than is due from it.	
Chapter 12 Common pleas shall not follow our court, but shall be held in some fixed place.	
Chapter 13 Recognitions of novel disseisin and of mort d'ancestor shall not be held elsewhere than in the counties to which they relate, and in this manner — we, or, if we should be out of the realm, our chief justiciar, will send justices through each county once a year, who with knights of the counties shall hold the said assizes in the counties, and those which cannot on that visit be determined in the county to which	

Magna Carta 1215 cont'd	Magna Carta 1216 cont'd
on the day and in the place of meeting of the county court.	on the day and in the place of meeting of the county court.
Chapter 19	*Chapter 14*
And if the said assizes cannot all be held on the day of the county court, there shall stay behind as many of the knights and freeholders who were present at the county court on that day as are necessary for the sufficient making of judgments, according to the amount of business to be done.	And if the said assizes cannot all be held on the day of the county court, there shall stay behind as many of the knights and freeholders who were present at the county court on that day as are necessary for the sufficient making of judgments, according to the amount of business to be done.

Magna Carta 1225 cont'd	Notes cont'd
they relate by the said justices sent to hold the said assizes shall be determined by them elsewhere on their circuit, and those which cannot be determined by them because of difficulty over certain articles shall be referred to our justices of the bench and determined there.	

Magna Carta 1215 cont'd	Magna Carta 1216 cont'd
Chapter 20	*Chapter 15*
A free man shall not be amerced for a trivial offence except in accordance with the degree of the offence, and for a grave offence he shall be amerced in accordance with its gravity, yet saving his way of living; and a merchant in the same way, saving his stock-in-trade; and a villein shall be amerced in the same way, saving his means of livelihood – if they have fallen into our mercy: and none of the aforesaid amercements shall be imposed except by the oath of good men of the neighbourhood.	A free man shall not be amerced for a trivial offence except in accordance with the degree of the offence, and for a grave offence in accordance with its gravity, yet saving his way of living; and a merchant in the same way, saving his stock-in-trade; and a villein shall be amerced in the same way, saving his means of livelihood; if he has fallen into our mercy: and none of the aforesaid amercements shall be imposed except by the oath of good and law-worthy men of the neighbourhood.

Magna Carta 1225 cont'd	Notes cont'd

Chapter 14

Assizes of darrein presentment shall always be held before the justices of the bench and determined there.

Chapter 15

A free man shall not be amerced for a trivial offence except in accordance with the degree of the offence and for a grave offence in accordance with its gravity, yet saving his way of living; and a merchant in the same way, saving his stock-in-trade; and a villein other than one of our own shall be amerced in the same way, saving his means of livelihood; if he has fallen into our mercy: and none of the aforesaid amercements shall be imposed except by the oath of good and law-worthy men of the neighbourhood.

Magna Carta 1215 cont'd	Magna Carta 1216 cont'd
Chapter 21	*Chapter 16*
Earls and barons shall not be amerced except by their peers, and only in accordance with the degree of the offence.	Earls and barons shall not be amerced except by their peers, and only in accordance with the degree of the offence.
Chapter 22	*Chapter 17*
No clerk shall be amerced in respect of his lay holding except after the manner of the others aforesaid and not according to the amount of ecclesiastical benefice.	No clerk shall be amerced except after the fashion of the aforesaid and not according to the amount of his ecclesiastical benefice.
Chapter 23	*Chapter 18*
No vill or individual shall be compelled to make bridges at river banks, except those who from of old are legally bound to do so.	No vill or individual shall be compelled to make bridges at river banks, except one who from of old is legally bound to do so.

Magna Carta 1225 cont'd	Notes cont'd
Chapter 15 (A) Earls and barons shall not be amerced except by their peers, and only in accordance with the degree of the offence.	
Chapter 15 (B) No ecclesiastical person shall be amerced according to the amount of his ecclesiastical benefice but in accordance with his lay holding and in accordance with the degree of the offence.	
Chapter 16 (A) No vill or individual shall be compelled to make bridges at river banks, except one who from of old is legally bound to do so.	
Chapter 16 (B) No river bank shall henceforth be made a preserve, except	

Magna Carta 1215 cont'd	Magna Carta 1216 cont'd
Chapter 24	*Chapter 19*
No sheriff, constable, coroners, or others of our bailiffs, shall hold pleas of our crown.	No sheriff, constable, coroners, or others of our bailiffs shall hold pleas of our crown.
Chapter 25[11]	
All counties, hundreds, wapentakes and trithings shall be at the old rents without any additional payment, except our demesne manors.	
Chapter 26	*Chapter 20*
If anyone holding a lay fief of us dies and our sheriff or bailiff shows our letters patent of summons for a debt that the deceased owed us, it shall be lawful for our sheriff or bailiff	If anyone holding a lay fief of us dies and our sheriff or bailiff shows our letters patent of summons for a debt that the deceased owed us, it shall be lawful for our sheriff or bailiff

Magna Carta 1225 cont'd	Notes cont'd
those which were preserves in the time of king Henry, our grandfather, in the same places and for the same periods as they used to be in his day.	
Chapter 17 No sheriff, constable, coroners, or others of our bailiffs shall hold pleas of our crown.	
	11. This chapter, 'on the customs of the counties', was one of those deemed to be 'important yet doubtful', and dropped from MC 1216 and all subsequent versions of the Charter (see MC 1216 Chapter 42 below).
Chapter 18 If anyone holding a lay fief of us dies and our sheriff or bailiff shows our letters patent of summons for a debt that the deceased owed us, it shall be lawful for our sheriff or bailiff	

Magna Carta 1215 cont'd

to attach and make a list of
chattels of the deceased found
upon the lay fief to the value
of that debt under the supervision of law-worthy men,
provided that none of the
chattels shall be removed until
the debt which is manifest has
been paid to us in full; and the
residue shall be left to the
executors for carrying out the
will of the deceased. And if
nothing is owing to us from
him, all the chattels shall
accrue to the deceased, saving
to his wife and children their
reasonable shares.

Chapter 27[12]

If any free man dies without
leaving a will, his chattels shall
be distributed by his nearest
kinsfolk and friends under the
supervision of the church,
saving to every one the debts
which the deceased owed him.

Magna Carta 1216 cont'd

to attach and make a list of
chattels of the deceased found
upon the lay fief to the value
of that debt under the supervision of law-worthy men,
provided that none of the
chattels shall be removed until
the debt which is manifest has
been paid to us in full; and the
residue shall be left to the
executors for carrying out the
will of the deceased. And if
nothing is owing to us from
him, all the chattels shall
accrue to the deceased, saving
to his wife and his children
their reasonable shares.

Magna Carta 1225 cont'd	Notes cont'd
to attach and make a list of chattels of the deceased found upon the lay fief to the value of that debt under the supervision of law-worthy men, provided that none of the chattels shall be removed until the debt which is manifest has been paid to us in full; and the residue shall be left to the executors for carrying out the will of the deceased. And if nothing is owing to us from him, all the chattels shall accrue to the deceased, saving to his wife and his children their reasonable shares.	

12. This chapter, 'on debts of Jews and others', was one of those deemed to be 'important yet doubtful', and dropped from MC 1216 and all subsequent versions of the Charter (see MC 1216 Chapter 42 below).

Magna Carta 1215 cont'd	Magna Carta 1216 cont'd
Chapter 28	*Chapter 21*
No constable or other bailiff of ours shall take anyone's corn or other chattels unless he pays on the spot in cash for them or can delay payment by arrangement with the seller.	No constable or his bailiff shall take the corn or other chattels of anyone who is not of the vill where the castle is situated unless he pays on the spot in cash for them or can delay payment by arrangement with the seller; if the seller is of the vill, he shall be bound to pay within three weeks.
Chapter 29	*Chapter 22*
No constable shall compel any knight to give money instead of castle-guard if he is willing to do the guard himself or through another good man, if for some good reason he cannot do it himself; and if we lead or send him on military service, he shall be excused guard in proportion to the time that because of us he has been on service.	No constable shall compel any knight to give money instead of castle-guard if he is willing to do it himself or through another good man, if for some good reason he cannot do it himself; and if we lead or send him on military service, he shall be excused guard in proportion to the time that because of us he has been on service.

Magna Carta 1225 cont'd	Notes cont'd
Chapter 19 No constable or his bailiff shall take the corn or other chattels of anyone who is not of the vill where the castle is situated unless he pays on the spot in cash for them or can delay payment by arrangement with the seller; if the seller is of that vill he shall pay within forty days.	
Chapter 20 No constable shall compel any knight to give money instead of castle-guard if he is willing to do it himself or through another good man, if for some good reason he cannot do it himself; and if we lead or send him on military service, he shall be excused guard in respect of the fief for which he did service in the army in proportion to the time that because of us he has been on service.	

Magna Carta 1215 cont'd	Magna Carta 1216 cont'd
Chapter 30	*Chapter 23*
No sheriff, or bailiff of ours, or anyone else shall take the horses or carts of any free man for transport work save with the agreement of that freeman.	No sheriff, or bailiff of ours, or other person shall take anyone's horses or carts for transport work unless he pays for them at the old-established rates, namely at ten pence a day for a cart with two horses and fourteen pence a day for a cart with three horses.
Chapter 31	*Chapter 24*
Neither we nor our bailiffs will take, for castles or other works of ours, timber which is not ours, except with the agreement of him whose timber it is.	Neither we nor our bailiffs will take, for castles or other works of ours, timber which is not ours, except with the agreement of him whose timber it is.
Chapter 32	*Chapter 25*
We will not hold for more than a year and a day the	We will not hold for more than a year and a day the

Magna Carta 1225 cont'd	Notes cont'd
Chapter 21 No sheriff, or bailiff of ours, or other person shall take anyone's horses or carts for transport work unless he pays for them at the old-established rates, namely at ten pence a day for a cart with two horses and fourteen pence a day for a cart with three horses. No demesne cart of any ecclesiastical person or knight or of any lady shall be taken by the aforesaid bailiffs.	
Chapter 21 Neither we nor our bailiffs nor others will take, for castles or other works of ours, timber which is not ours, except with the agreement of him whose timber it is.	
Chapter 22 We will not hold for more than a year and a day the	

Magna Carta 1215 cont'd	Magna Carta 1216 cont'd
lands of those convicted of felony, and then the lands shall be handed over to the lords of the fiefs.	lands of those convicted of felony, and then the lands shall be handed over to the lords of the fiefs.
Chapter 33 Henceforth all the fish-weirs shall be cleared completely from the Thames and the Medway and throughout all England, except along the sea coast.	*Chapter 26* Henceforth all fish-weirs shall be cleared completely from the Thames and the Medway and throughout all England, except along the sea coast.
Chapter 34 The writ called Praecipe shall not in future be issued to anyone in respect of any holding whereby a free man may lose his court.	*Chapter 27* The writ called Praecipe shall not in future be issued to anyone in respect of any holding whereby a free man may lose his court.
Chapter 35 Let there be one measure for wine throughout our kingdom, and one measure for ale, and one measure for corn, namely 'the London quarter'; and one	*Chapter 28* Let there be one measure for wine throughout our kingdom, and one measure for ale, and one measure for corn, namely 'the London quarter'; and one

Magna Carta 1225 cont'd	Notes cont'd
lands of those convicted of felony, and then the lands shall be handed over to the lords of the fiefs.	
Chapter 23 Henceforth all fish-weirs shall be cleared completely from the Thames and the Medway and throughout all England, except along the sea coast.	
Chapter 24 The writ called Praecipe shall not in future be issued to anyone in respect of any holding whereby a free man may lose his court.	
Chapter 25 Let there be one measure for wine throughout our kingdom, and one measure for ale, and one measure for corn, namely 'the London quarter'; and one	

Magna Carta 1215 cont'd	Magna Carta 1216 cont'd
width for cloths whether dyed, russet, or halberget, namely two ells within the selvedges. Let it be the same with weights as with measures.	width for cloths whether dyed, russet or halberget, namely two ells within the selvedges. Let it be the same with weights as with measures.

Chapter 36

Nothing shall be given or taken in future for the writ of inquisition of life or limbs: instead it shall be granted free of charge and not refused.

Chapter 29

Nothing shall be given in future for the writ of inquisition of life or limbs: instead, it shall be granted free of charge and not refused.

Chapter 37

If anyone holds of us by fee-farm, by socage, or by burgage, and holds land of another by knight service, we will not, by reason of that fee-farm, socage, or burgage, have the wardship of his heir or of land of his that is of the fief of the other; nor will we have custody of the fee-farm, socage, or burgage, unless

Chapter 30

If anyone holds of us by fee-farm, by socage, or by burgage, and holds land of another by knight service, we will not, by reason of that fee-farm, socage, or burgage, have the wardship of his heir or of land of his that is of the fief of the other; nor will we have cusody of the fee-farm, socage, or burgage, unless

Magna Carta 1225 cont'd	Notes cont'd
width for cloths whether dyed, russet or halberget, namely two ells within the selvedges. Let it be the same with weights as with measures.	
Chapter 26 Nothing shall be given in future for the writ of inquisition by him who seeks an inquisition of life or limbs: instead, it shall be granted free of charge and not refused.	
Chapter 27 If anyone holds of us by fee-farm, by socage, or by burgage, and holds land of another by knight service, we will not, by reason of that fee-farm, socage or burgage, have the wardship of his heir or of land of his that is of the fief of the other; nor will we have custody of the fee-farm, socage, or burgage, unless	

Magna Carta 1215 cont'd	Magna Carta 1216 cont'd
such fee-farm owes knight service. We will not have custody of anyone's heir or land which he holds of another by knight service by reason of any petty serjeanty which he holds of us by the service of rendering to us knives or arrows or the like.	such fee-farm owes knight service. We will not have custody of anyone's heir or land which he holds of another by knight service by reason of any petty serjeanty which he holds of us by the service of rendering to us knives or arrows or the like.

Chapter 38

No bailiff shall in future put anyone to trial upon his own bare word, without reliable witnesses produced for this purpose.

Chapter 31

No bailiff shall in future put anyone to trial upon his own bare word without reliable witnesses produced for this purpose.

Chapter 39

No free man shall be arrested or imprisoned or disseised or outlawed or exiled or in any way victimised, neither will we attack him or send anyone to attack him, except by the lawful judgment of his peers or by the law of the land.

Chapter 32

No free man shall be arrested or imprisoned or disseised or outlawed or exiled or victimised in any other way, neither will we attack him or send anyone to attack him, except by the lawful judgment of his peers or by the law of the land.

Magna Carta 1225 cont'd	Notes cont'd
such fee-farm owes knight service. We will not have custody of anyone's heir or land which he holds of another by knight service by reason of any petty serjeanty which he holds of us by the service of rendering to us knives or arrows or the like.	

Chapter 28	
No bailiff shall in future put anyone to manifest trial or to oath upon his own bare word without reliable witnesses produced for this purpose.	

Chapter 29 (A)	
No free man shall in future be arrested or imprisoned or disseised of his freehold, liberties or free customs, or outlawed or exiled or victimised in any other way, neither will we attack him or send anyone to attack him, except	

Magna Carta 1215 cont'd | Magna Carta 1216 cont'd

Chapter 40

To no one will we sell, to no
one will we refuse or delay
right or justice.

Chapter 33

To no one will we sell, to no
one will we refuse or delay
right or justice.

Chapter 41

All merchants shall be able to
go out of and come into
England safely and securely
and stay and travel throughout
England, as well by land as by
water, for buying and selling
by the ancient and right
customs free from all evil tolls,
except in time of war and if
they are of the land that is at
war with us. And if such are
found in our land at the beginning of a war, they shall be
attached, without injury to
their persons or goods, until
we, or our chief justiciar,

Chapter 34

All merchants, unless they
have been publicly prohibited
beforehand, shall be able to go
out of and come into England
safely and securely and stay
and travel throughout
England, as well by land as by
water, for buying and selling
by the ancient and right
customs free from all evil tolls,
except in time of war and if
they are of the land that is at
war with us. And if such are
found in our land at the beginning of a war, they shall be
attached, without injury to

Magna Carta 1225 cont'd	Notes cont'd
by the lawful judgment of his peers or by the law of the land.	

Chapter 29 (B)

To no one will we sell, to no one will we refuse or delay right or justice.

Chapter 30

All merchants, unless they have been publicly prohibited beforehand, shall be able to go out of and come into England safely and securely and stay and travel throughout England, as well by land as by water, for buying and selling by the ancient and right customs free from all evil tolls, except in time of war and if they are of the land that is at war with us. And if such are found in our land at the beginning of a war, they shall be attached without injury to

Magna Carta 1215 cont'd	Magna Carta 1216 cont'd
know how merchants of our land are treated who were found in the land at war with us when war broke out; and if ours are safe there, the others shall be safe in our land.	their persons or goods, until we, or our chief justiciar, know how merchants of our land are treated who were found in the land at war with us when war broke out; and if ours are safe there, the others shall be safe in our land.

Chapter 42[13]

It shall be lawful in future for anyone, without prejudicing the allegiance due to us, to leave our kingdom and return safely and securely by land and water, save, in the public interest, for a short period in time of war – except for those imprisoned or outlawed in accordance with the law of the kingdom and natives of a land that is at war with us and merchants (who shall be treated as aforesaid).

Magna Carta 1225 cont'd	Notes cont'd
their persons or goods, until we, or our chief justiciar, know how merchants of our land are treated who were found in the land at war with us when war broke out; and if ours are safe there, the others shall be safe in our land.	
	13. This chapter, 'on freedom to leave and return to our kingdom' was one of those deemed to be 'important yet doubtful', and dropped from MC 1216 and all subsequent versions of the Charter (see MC 1216 Chapter 42 below).

Magna Carta 1215 cont'd	Magna Carta 1216 cont'd
Chapter 43	*Chapter 35*
If anyone who holds of some escheat such as the honour of Wallingford, Nottingham, Boulogne, Lancaster, or of eschants which are in our hands and are baronres dies, its heir shall give no other relief and do no other service to us than he would have done to the baron if that barony had been in the baron's hands; and we will hold it in the same manner in which the baron held it.	If anyone who holds of some escheat such as the honour of Wallingford, Nottingham, Boulogne, Lancaster, or of other escheats which are in our hands and are baronies dies, his heir shall give no other relief and do no other service to us than he would have done to the baron if that land had been in the baron's hands; and we will hold it in the same manner in which the barons held it.
Chapter 44[14]	*Chapter 36*[14]
Men who live outside the forest need not henceforth come before our justices of the forest upon a general	Men who live outside the forest need not henceforth come before our justices of the forest upon a general

Magna Carta 1225 cont'd	Notes cont'd

Chapter 31

If anyone who holds of some escheat such as the honour of Wallingford, Boulogne, Nottingham, Lancaster, or of other escheats which are in our hands and are baronies dies, his heir shall give no other relief and do no other service to us than he would have done to the baron if that had been in the baron's hands; and we will hold it in the same manner in which the baron held it. Nor will we by reason of such a barony or escheat have any escheat or wardship of any men of ours unless he who held the barony or escheat held in chief of us elsewhere.

14. *This chapter was omitted after MC 1216, having been transferred to the separate Charter of the Forest, 1217.*

Magna Carta 1215 cont'd	Magna Carta 1216 cont'd
summons, unless they are impleaded or are sureties for any person or persons who are attached for forest offences.	summons, unless they are impleaded or are sureties for any person or persons who are attached for forest offences.

Chapter 45[15]

We will not make justices, constables, sheriffs, or bailiffs save of such as know the law of the kingdom and mean to observe it well.

Chapter 46	*Chapter 37*
All barons who have founded abbeys for which they have charters of the kings of England or ancient tenure	All barons who have founded abbeys for which they have charters of the kings of England or ancient tenure

Magna Carta 1225 cont'd	Notes cont'd
Chapter 29 No free man shall henceforth give or sell to anyone more of his land than will leave enough for the full service due from the fief to be rendered to the lord of the fief.	
	15. This chapter, 'on the customs of the counties', was one of those deemed to be 'important yet doubtful', and dropped from MC 1216 and all subsequent versions of the Charter (see MC 1216 Chapter 42 below).
Chapter 33 All patrons of abbeys who have charters of advowson of the kings of England or ancient tenure or possession	

Magna Carta 1215 cont'd	Magna Carta 1216 cont'd
shall have the custody of them during vacancies, as they ought to have.	shall have the custody of them during vacancies, as they ought to have *and as it is made clear above*.
Chapter 47[16] All forests that have been made forest in our time shall be immediately disafforested; and so be it done with river-banks that have been made preserves by us in our time.	*Chapter 38*[16] All forests that were made forest in the time of King John, our father, shall be immediately disafforested; and so be it done with river-banks that were made preserves by the same J. in his time.
Chapter 48[17] All evil customs connected with forests and warrens, foresters and warreners, sheriffs and their officials, river-banks and their wardens shall immediately be inquired into in each county by twelve sworn knights of the same county who are to be chosen by good men of the same county, and within forty days of the completion of the	

Magna Carta 1225 cont'd	Notes cont'd
shall have the custody of them during vacancies, as they ought to have and as is made clear above.	
	16. After MC 1216, this chapter was split into two. The section relating to the forest was transferred to the separate Charter of the Forest, 1217; the remainder on riverbanks became MC 1225 Chapter 16 (B).
	17. This chapter, 'on forests and foresters, warrens and warreners' and 'on river-banks and their wardens' was one of those deemed to be 'important yet doubtful', and dropped from MC 1216; but the returns of the county juries, obtained in pursuance of this chapter, were almost certainly used in the drafting of the Charter of the Forest, 1217.

Magna Carta 1215 cont'd	Magna Carta 1216 cont'd
inquiry shall be utterly abolished by them so as never to be restored, provided that we, or our justiciar if we are not in England, know of it first.	

Chapter 49[18]

We will immediately return all hostages and charters given to us by Englishmen, as security for peace or faithful service.

Chapter 50[19]

We will remove completely from office the relations of Gerard de Athée so that in future they shall have no office in England, namely Engelard de Cigogné, Peter and Guy and Andrew de Chanceaux, Guy de Cigogné, Geoffrey de Martigny and his brothers, Philip Marc and his brothers and his nephew Geoffrey, and all their following.

Magna Carta 1225 cont'd	Notes cont'd
	18. This chapter was silently omitted in 1216 as both contentious and specific to the political situation of 1215.
	19. This chapter was silently omitted in 1216 as both contentious and specific to the political situation of 1215.

Magna Carta 1215 cont'd	Magna Carta 1216 cont'd

Chapter 51[20]

As soon as peace is restored we will remove from the kingdom all foreign knights, cross-bowmen, serjeants, and mercenaries, who have come with horses and arms to the detriment of the kingdom.

Chapter 52[21]

If anyone has been disseised or kept out of his lands, castles, franchises or his right by us without legal judgment of his peers, we will immediately restore them to him: and if a dispute arises over this, then let it be decided by the judgment of the twenty-five barons who are mentioned below in the clause for securing the peace: for all the things, however, which anyone has been disseised or kept out of without the lawful judgment of his peers by king Henry, our father, or by king

Magna Carta 1225 cont'd	Notes cont'd
	20. This chapter was silently omitted in 1216 as both contentious and specific to the political situation of 1215.
	21. This chapter was silently omitted in 1216 as both contentious and specific to the political situation of 1215.

Magna Carta 1215 cont'd	Magna Carta 1216 cont'd
Richard, our brother, which we have in our hand or are held by others, to whom we are bound to warrant them, we will have the usual period of respite of crusaders, excepting those things about which a plea was started or an inquest made by our command before we took the cross; when however we return from our pilgrimage, or if by any chance we do not go on it, we will at once do full justice therein.	

Chapter 53[22]

We will give the same respite, and in the same manner, in the doing of justice in the matter of the disafforesting or retaining of the forests which Henry our father or Richard our brother afforested, and in the matter of wardship of lands which are of the fief of another, wardships of which sort we

Magna Carta 1225 cont'd	Notes cont'd
	22. This chapter was silently omitted in 1216 as both contentious and specific to the political situation of 1215.

Magna Carta 1215 cont'd	Magna Carta 1216 cont'd
have hitherto had by reason of a fief which anyone held of us by knight service, and in the matter of abbeys founded on the fief of another, not on a fief of our own, in which the lord of the fief claims he has a right; and when we have returned, or if we do not set out on our pilgrimage, we will at once do full justice to those who complain of these things.	
Chapter 54	*Chapter 39*
No one shall be arrested or imprisoned upon the appeal of a woman for the death of anyone except her husband.	No one shall be arrested or imprisoned upon the appeal of a woman for the death of anyone except her husband.
Chapter 55[23]	
All fines made with us unjustly and against the law of the land, and all amercements imposed unjustly and against the law of the land, shall be entirely remitted, or else let them be	

Magna Carta 1225 cont'd	Notes cont'd
Chapter 34	
No one shall be arrested or imprisoned upon the appeal of a woman for the death of anyone except her husband.	
	23. *This chapter was silently omitted in 1216 as both contentious and specific to the political situation of 1215.*

Magna Carta 1215 cont'd | Magna Carta 1216 cont'd

settled by the judgment of
twenty-five barons who are
mentioned below in the clause
for securing the peace, or by
the judgment of the majority
of the same, along with the
aforesaid Stephen, archbishop
of Canterbury, if he can be
present, and such others as he
may wish to associate with
himself for this purpose, and if
he cannot be present the business shall nevertheless proceed
without him, provided that if
any one or more of the aforesaid twenty-five barons are in
a like suit, they shall be
removed from the judgment of
the case in question, and others
chosen, sworn and put in their
place by the rest of the same
twenty-five for this case only.

Chapter 56[24]

If we have disseised or kept
out Welshmen from lands or
liberties or other things

Chapter 40[24]

And if king J. our father
disseised or kept out
Welshmen from lands or

Magna Carta 1225 cont'd

Notes cont'd

24. *This chapter was silently omitted after MC 1216 as specific to the political situation of 1215-16.*

Magna Carta 1215 cont'd

without the legal judgment of
their peers in England or in
Wales, they shall be immediately restored to them; and if a
dispute arises over this, then
let it be decided in the March
by the judgment of their peers
– for holdings in England
according to the law of
England, for holdings in
Wales according to the law of
Wales, and for holdings in the
March according to the law of
the March. Welshmen shall do
the same to us and ours.

Chapter 57[25]

For all the things, however,
which any Welshmen was
disseised of or kept out of
without the lawful judgment
of his peers by king Henry,
our father, or king Richard,
our brother, which we have in
our hand or which are held
by others, to whom we are

Magna Carta 1216 cont'd

liberties or other things
without the legal judgment of
their peers in England or in
Wales, they shall be immediately restored to them; and if a
dispute arises over this, then
let it be decided in the March
by the judgment of their peers
– for holdings in England
according to the law of
England, for holdings in
Wales according to the laws of
Wales and for holdings in the
March according to the law of
the March. Welshmen shall do
the same to us and ours.

Magna Carta 1225 cont'd	Notes cont'd
	25. This chapter was silently omitted in 1216 as both contentious and specific to the political situation of 1215.

Magna Carta 1215 cont'd	Magna Carta 1216 cont'd

bound to warrant them, we will have the usual period of respite of crusaders, excepting those things about which a plea was started or an inquest made by our command before we took the cross; when however we return, or if by any chance we do not set out on our pilgrimage, we will at once do full justice to them in accordance with the laws of the Welsh and the foresaid regions.

Chapter 58[26]

We will give back at once the son of Llywelyn and all the hostages from Wales and the charters that were handed over to us as security for peace.

Chapter 59[27]

We will act toward Alexander, king of the Scots, concerning the return of his sisters and

Magna Carta 1225 cont'd	Notes cont'd
	26. This chapter was silently omitted in 1216 as both contentious and specific to the political situation of 1215.
	27. This chapter was silently omitted in 1216 as both contentious and specific to the political situation of 1215.

Magna Carta 1215 cont'd | Magna Carta 1216 cont'd

hostages and concerning his franchises and his right in the same manner in which we act towards our other barons of England, unless it ought to be otherwise by the charters which we have from William his father, formerly king of the Scots, and this shall be determined by the judgment of his peers in our court.

Magna Carta 1225 cont'd	Notes cont'd

Chapter 35[28]

No county court shall in future be held more often than once a month and where a greater interval has been customary let it be greater. Nor shall any sheriff or bailiff make his tourn through the hundred save twice a year (and then only in the due and accustomed place), that is to say, once after Easter and again after Michaelmas. And view of frankpledge shall be held then at the Michaelmas

28. *Provisions relating to 'the customs of the counties' had been deferred in MC 1216; here they are re-enacted in part.*

Magna Carta 1215 cont'd | Magna Carta 1216 cont'd

Magna Carta 1225 cont'd | Notes cont'd

term without interference, that is to say, so that each has his liberties which he had and was accustomed to have in the time of king Henry our grandfather or which he has since acquired. View of frankpledge shall be held in this manner, namely, that our peace be kept, that a tithing be kept full as it used to be, and that the sheriff shall not look for opportunities for exactions but be satisfied with what a sheriff used to get from holding his view in the time of king Henry our grandfather.

Chapter 36[29]

It shall not in future be lawful for anyone to give land of his to any religious house in such a way that he gets it back again as a tenant of that house. Nor shall it be lawful for any religious house to receive anyone's land to hand

29. This chapter had been introduced for the first time in the MC re-issue of 1217.

Magna Carta 1215 cont'd	Magna Carta 1216 cont'd
Chapter 60	*Chapter 41*
All these aforesaid customs and liberties which we have granted to be observed in our kingdom as far as it pertains	All these aforesaid customs and liberties which we have granted to be observed in our kingdom as far as it pertains

Magna Carta 1225 cont'd

Notes cont'd

it back to him as a tenant.
And if in future anyone does
give land of his in this way to
any religious house and he is
convicted of it, his gift shall
be utterly quashed and the
land shall be forfeit to the lord
of the fief concerned.

Chapter 37[30]

Scutage shall be taken in future
as it used to be taken in the
time of king Henry our grandfather. And let there be saved
to archbishops, bishops, abbots,
priors, Templars, Hospitallers,
earls, barons and all other
persons, ecclesiastical and
secular, the liberties and free
customs they had previously.

30. *Provisions relating to 'the
assessing of scutage and aids' had
been deferred in MC 1216; here they
are re-enacted in part.*

Chapter 38

All these aforesaid customs
and liberties which we have
granted to be observed in our
kingdom as far as it pertains

Magna Carta 1215 cont'd

Magna Carta 1216 cont'd

to us towards our men, all of
our kingdom, clerks as well as
laymen, shall observe as far as
it pertains to them towards
their men.

to us towards our men, all of
our kingdom, clerks as well as
laymen, shall observe as far as
it pertains to them towards
their men.

Chapter 61[31]

Since, moreover, for God and
the betterment of our kingdom
and for the better allaying of
the discord that has arisen
between us and our barons we
have granted all these things
aforesaid, wishing them to
enjoy the use of them unimpaired and unshaken for ever,
we give and grant them
under-written security, namely,
that the barons shall choose
any twenty-five barons of the
kingdom they wish, who must
with all their might observe,
hold and cause to be observed,
the peace and liberties which
we have granted and
confirmed to them by this
present charters of ours, so

Magna Carta 1225 cont'd	Notes cont'd
to us towards our men, all of our kingdom, clerks as well as laymen, shall observe as far as it pertains to them towards their men.	

31. This, the 'forma securitatis', was silently omitted in MC 1216 as both contentious and specific to the political situation in 1215.

Magna Carta 1215 cont'd | Magna Carta 1216 cont'd

that if we, or our justiciar, or
our bailiffs or any one of our
servants offend in any way
against anyone or transgress
any of the articles of the peace
or the security and the offence
be notified to four of the
aforesaid twenty-five barons,
those four barons shall come
to us, or to our justiciar if we
are out of the kingdom, and,
laying the transgression before
us, shall petition us to have
that transgression corrected
without delay. And if we do
not correct the transgression,
or if we are out of the
kingdom, the aforesaid four
barons shall refer that case to
the rest of the twenty-five
barons and those twenty-five
barons together with the
community of the whole land
shall distrain and distress us in
every way they can, namely,
by seizing castles, lands,
possessions, and in such other
ways as they can, saving our

Magna Carta 1225 cont'd

Notes cont'd

Magna Carta 1215 cont'd | Magna Carta 1216 cont'd

person and the persons of our
queen and our children, until,
in their opinion, amends have
been made; and when amends
have been made, they shall
obey us as they did before.
And let anyone in the land
who wishes take an oath to
obey the orders of the said
twenty-five barons for the
execution of all the aforesaid
matters, and with them to
distress us as much as he can,
and we publicly and freely
give anyone leave to take the
oath who wishes to take it and
we will never prohibit anyone
from taking it. Indeed, all
those in the land who are
unwilling of themselves and of
their own accord to take an
oath to the twenty-five barons
to help them to distrain and
distress us, we will make them
take the oath as aforesaid at
our command. And if any of
the twenty-five barons dies or
leaves the country or is in any

Magna Carta 1225 cont'd | Notes cont'd

Magna Carta 1215 cont'd | Magna Carta 1216 cont'd

other way prevented from
carrying out the things aforesaid, the rest of the aforesaid
twenty-five barons shall
choose as they think fit
another one in his place, and
he shall take the oath like the
rest. In all matters the execution of which is committed to
these twenty-five barons, if it
should happen that these
twenty-five are present yet
disagree among themselves
about anything, or if some of
those summoned will not or
cannot be present, that shall be
held as fixed and established
which the majority of those
present ordained or
commanded, exactly as if all
the twenty-five had consented
to it; and the said twenty-five
shall swear that they will
faithfully observe all the
things aforesaid and will do all
they can to get them observed.
And we will procure nothing
from anyone, either personally

Magna Carta 1225 cont'd | Notes cont'd

Magna Carta 1215 cont'd	Magna Carta 1216 cont'd
or through anyone else, whereby any of these concessions and liberties might be revoked or diminished; and if any such thing is procured, let it be void and null, and we will never use it either personally or through another.	

Chapter 62[32]

And we have fully remitted and pardoned to everyone all the ill-will, indignation and rancour that have arisen between us and our men, clergy and laity, from the time of the quarrel. Furthermore, we have fully remitted to all, clergy and laity, and as far as pertains to us have completely forgiven, all trespasses occasioned by the same quarrel between Easter in the sixteenth year of our reign and the restoration of peace. And, besides, we have caused to be made for them letters testimo-

Magna Carta 1225 cont'd	Notes cont'd
	32. Silently omitted in MC 1216 as specific to political situation of 1215.

Magna Carta 1215 cont'd | Magna Carta 1216 cont'd

nial patent of the lord Stephen archbishop of Canterbury, of the lord Henry archbishop of Dublin and of the aforementioned bishops and of master Pandulf about this security and the aforementioned concessions.

Chapter 63

Wherefore we wish and firmly enjoin that the English church shall be free, and that the men in our kingdom shall have and hold all the aforesaid liberties, rights and concessions well and peacefully, freely and quietly, fully and completely, for themselves and their heirs from us and our heirs, in all matters and in all places for ever, as is aforesaid. An oath, moreover, has been taken, as well on our part as on the part of the barons, that all these things aforesaid shall be observed in good faith and

Chapter 42[33]

However, because there were certain articles contained in the former charter which seemed important yet doubtful, namely On the assessing of scutage and aids, On debts of Jews and others, On freedom to leave and return to our kingdom, On forests and foresters, warrens and warreners, On the customs of counties, and On river-banks and their wardens, the above-mentioned prelates and magnates have agreed to these being deferred until we have fuller counsel, when we

Magna Carta 1225 cont'd	Notes cont'd

Chapter 39

In return for this grant and gift of these liberties and of the other liberties contained in our charter on the liberties of the forest, the archbishops, bishops, abbots, priors, earls, barons, knights, freeholders and all of our realm have given us a fifteenth part of all their movables.[34] We have also granted to them for us and our heirs that neither we nor our heirs will procure anything whereby the liberties contained in this charter shall be infringed or weakened; and if any thing contrary to this is

33. This chapter reads like a classic exercise in bureaucratic 'parking'. Actually, many of the deferred chapters were eventually re-enacted after the promised further consideration - whether in the Charter of the Forest or subsequent versions of the Charter. (See MC 1225 chapters 28, 37).

34. 'In return for this ... all their movables'. This clause, which recorded that Henry III had reissued the Charter in return for a grant of taxation, turned the Charter from an act of baronial coercion, as in 1215, into a compact, freely entered into on both sides, between the king and 'all of our realm'. It also laid the foundations of parliament and the practice of granting supply in return for the redress of grievances.

Magna Carta 1215 cont'd

Magna Carta 1216 cont'd

without evil disposition. Witness the above-mentioned and many others. Given by our hand in the meadow which is called Runnymede between Windsor and Staines on the fifteenth day of June, in the seventeenth year of our reign.

will, most fully in these as well as other matters that have to be amended, do what is for the common good and the peace and estate of ourselves and our kingdom. Because we have not yet a seal, we have had the present charter sealed with the seals of our venerable father, the lord Gualo cardinal priest of St Martin, legate of the apostolic see, and William Marshal earl of Pembroke, ruler of us and of our kingdom.[35] Witness all the aforementioned and many others. Given by the hands of the aforesaid lord, the legate, and William Marshal earl of Pembroke at Bristol on the twelfth day of November in the first year of our reign.

Magna Carta 1225 cont'd

procured from anyone, it shall avail nothing and be held for nought.[36] These being witness:[37] the lord S. archbishop of Canterbury, E. of London, J. of Bath, P. of Winchester, H. of Lincoln, R. of Salisbury, B. of Rochester, W. of Worcester, J. of Ely, H. of Hereford, R. of Chichester and W. of Exeter, bishops; the abbot of St Albans, the abbot of Bury St Edmunds, the abbot of Battle, the abbot of St Augustine's, Canterbury, the abbot of Evesham, the abbot of Westminster, the abbot of Peterborough, the abbot of Reading, the abbot of Abingdon, the abbot of Malmesbury, the abbot of Winchcombe, the abbot of Hyde, the abbot of Chertsey, the abbot of Sherborne, the abbot of Cerne, the abbot of Abbotsbury, the abbot of Milton, the abbot of Selby, the abbot of Whitby, the abbot of

Notes cont'd

35. 'Because we have not yet a seal … ruler of us and of our kingdom'. The issuing of MC 1216 in the names of Gualo and Marshal and over their seals worked well in the circumstances of Henry III's minority. But in time it would raise insistent questions about the king's attitude to the Charter when he attained his majority.

36. 'We have also … be held for nought'. This clause, borrowed from MC 1215 chapter 61, sought to protect the Charter against the fact that the pope as England's overlord had not yet given his consent to the charter. This was made good by Pope Gregory IX in 1228.

37. 'These being witness'. In MC 1225 the king's councillors appear only as witnesses to the royal act of issuing and sealing the charter. This is in contrast to MC 1215 and MC 1216 when the councillors impel the issuing of the Charter by their advice.

Magna Carta 1225 cont'd

Cirencester, H. de Burgh the
justiciar, R. earl of Chester
and Lincoln, W. earl of
Salisbury, W. earl of Warenne,
G. de Clare earl of Gloucester
and Hertford, W. de Ferrers
earl of Derby, W. de
Mandeville earl of Essex, H. le
Bigod earl of Norfolk, W.
count of Aumale, H. earl of
Hereford, John the constable
of Chester, Robert de Ros,
Robert fitz Walter, Robert de
Vipont, William Brewer,
Richard de Munfichet, Peter
fitz Herbert, Matthew fitz
Herbert, William de Aubeney,
Robert Grelley, Reginald de
Braose, John of Monmouth,
John fitz Alan, Hugh de
Mortimer, Walter de
Beauchamp, William of St
John, Peter de Maulay, Brian
de Lisle, Thomas of Moulton,
Richard de Argentein,
Geoffrey de Neville, William
Mauduit, John de Balun.

Magna Carta 1225 cont'd

Given at Westminster on the
eleventh day of February in
the ninth year of our reign.

NOTES ON SOURCES

J.C. Holt, *Magna Carta* (Cambridge, 1st ed. 1965, 2nd ed. 1992) remains the classic account. I have drawn on it heavily, not only for its interpretations but also for its appendix of documents and photographs. *The Oxford Dictionary of National Biography* contains full and up-to-date (and often very well written) lives of all the principal Anglo-Norman actors in the drama. Once again, I have made heavy use of these, both for their sense of character and to shape the narrative.

For particular episodes I have, wherever possible, gone beyond these secondary works and used original sources in print. The account of the abortive 700th anniversary celebrations of 1915 comes from the Introduction to H. E. Malden, ed., *Magna Carta Commemoration Essays* (London, 1917).

Rigord's contemporary Latin *Life* of Philip Augustus, which first gives the king his surname, is translated into French in F. P. G. Guizot, ed., *Collection des Mémoires relatifs à l'Histoire de France* (Paris, 1825). The extracts from the Barnwell chronicler, generally regarded as the most authoritative contemporary account of John's reign, are taken from Holt, *Magna Carta*. There is a vigorous translation of Roger of Wendover, who gives a highly coloured, very hostile and now much-questioned view of John, by J. A. Giles, ed. and trans., *Roger of Wendover's Flowers of History* 2 vols. (London, 1849).

John's inaugural 'Constitution' is printed in T. Rymer, ed., *Foedera, Conventiones, Litterae* . . . new ed., vol. I, part 1, ed. A. Clarke and F. Holbrooke (Record Commission, 1816). My attention was drawn to it by D. A. Carpenter, 'Archbishop Langton and Magna Carta: his contribution, his doubts and his hypocrisy', *English Historical Review* 126 (2011). This important article has done much to alter my view of the Charters and, in particular, of the role that Stephen Langton did (and did not) play in their genesis.

The firm dating of the 'unknown charter' to the beginning of May 1215 and its interpretation as a riposte to John's initiatives of the 9th and 10th are largely my own going out on a limb. As is the emphasis on the technical term *consequentia*. But they do seem to make the best sense of the document.

My interpretation of Langton's role at Runnymede and the reading of chapter 1 of Magna Carta derive, once again, from Carpenter, 'Archbishop Langton and Magna Carta'.

My picture of the workings of the royal chancery and its dissemination of Magna Carta is based on Holt, *Magna Carta*. But much of the detail is supplied by N. Vincent's chapter on 'Why 1199?: Bureaucracy and Enrolment under John and his Contemporaries' in Adrian Jobson, ed., *English Government in the Thirteenth Century* (Martlesham, 2004).

Administrative history is rarely lively; this is and I have done my best to reflect it.

The materials for my account of chapter 61 of Magna Carta (the *forma securitatis*) and the treaty on the custody of London are likewise taken from Holt, *Magna Carta*. But I give them a novel emphasis. I stress the radical, proto-republican character both of the documents themselves and the way in which they were exploited by the baronial opposition. I also try to make the documents actors in the story by describing their physical appearance and the particular way in which they were written. In other words, by characterising them. Administrative history, as I have already noted, is seen as dull. It needn't be if the documents themselves are treated as artefacts.

The texts of the decisive papal interventions in Magna Carta are printed in F. M. Powicke, 'The Bull "Miramur plurimum" and a Letter to Archbishop Stephen Langton', *English Historical Review* 44 (1929). I follow the hints in Powicke, 'Alexander of St Albans, a literary muddle' in H. W. C. Davis, ed., *Essays in History Presented to Reginald Lane Poole* (Oxford, 1927) to reconstruct the other side of the coin in the intellectual career of an anti-papal clerical supporter of the baronial party. The story of Alexander's role as a royal propagandist during the Interdict forms an episode in Roger of Wendover; the intercessory letter written on his behalf when he had fallen on hard times is translated in T. Duffus Hardy, *A Description of the Close*

Rolls in the Tower of London (London, 1833). Powicke's suggestion that this latter farrago was written by the sober, scholarly Langton is very unlikely. Hence my alternative identification of Alexander himself as the author.

The text of the two 'writs' issued in the name of the Twenty-five appears in Holt, *Magna Carta*. But the interpretation of them as the administrative instruments of a proto-republican government is mine. As is the analysis of their 'diplomatics' – that is, of their formal features of address, place and date of issue.

Prince Louis's claim to the throne was summarised in his letter to the Abbot of St Augustine's, Canterbury, which William Thomas reproduced in his Chronicle printed in Roger Twysden, ed., *Historiae Anglicanae Scriptores Decem* (London, 1652). The letter is frequently mentioned. But, as far as I am aware, I am the first to analyse its assertions in full.

I have drawn directly on P. Meyer, ed., *L'Histoire de Guillaume le Maréchal*, 3 vols. (Paris, 1891-1901) for my account of its hero (and mine too, I suppose). The text of John's dictated will is reproduced and discussed in S. D. Church, 'King John's Testament and the Last Days of his Reign', *English Historical Review* 125 (2010).

For the definitive reissue of the Charter in 1225 and Langton's role in it, I have relied as ever on Carpenter, 'Archbishop Langton and Magna Carta'. The description of the solemn excommunication in 1253 of all infringers of

Magna Carta comes from J. A. Giles, ed. and trans., *Matthew Paris's English History* 3 vols. (London, 1852–4).

The contemporary verdict on the 1215 Magna Carta as the centrepiece of a revolutionary upheaval appears in a versified section of the Chronicle of Melrose Abbey in J. Stevenson, ed., *The Church Historians of England*, vol. IV part 1 (London, 1856).

The translation of the charters reproduced in the Appendix are from *English Historical Documents Volume 3*, edited by Harry Rothwell, published by Routledge.

ACKNOWLEDGEMENTS

The intellectual debts I have incurred in writing this book are acknowledged in the *Notes On Sources*. Apart, that is, from the most important, to which I shall return shortly.

Here instead it is my pleasant task to thank those who have helped me practically with the book's writing and production. The idea of the book was conceived in a series of conversations between Peter Robinson, my long-standing agent and friend, and Rupert Lancaster of Hodder & Stoughton. Both went on to prove deft midwives to the process of gestation and delivery. Maddy Price has overseen the copy editing and the production of proofs with a rare combination of efficiency and unflappable good humour. She and her assistant Rose Henry also went far beyond the call of duty in rekeying the three Charters of 1215, 1216 and 1225 for the comparative tabulation which concludes the book and caps the argument. Juliet Brightmore, Hodder's Picture Editor, researched the illustrations with taste, flair and sleuth-like skill. The result of her efforts is a book that looks as good as I hope it reads. My partner James Brown has, as usual, read each chapter as it was written; he also proofed the comparative table of Charters.

I am grateful to all of them for their care and scrutiny—though of course the responsibility for any remaining errors is mine alone.

Finally, however, I should like to return to the dedication which acknowledges a much older and deeper debt. The late Sir Geoffrey Elton taught me as an undergraduate in Cambridge in the 1960s and was subsequently my research supervisor there as well. We became close before we quarrelled very publicly and bitterly. The dedication is to make some small amends. It also acknowledges Elton's influence. His special subject class, where I first learned to think historically, was rigorously document-based. I have heard his voice and felt the rough edge of his tongue as I have written this, the most directly document-based of all my books, which stands or falls with what it has been possible to conjure from scraps of parchment and wax. 'Look at the form of the document', he would say. 'How is it addressed? How dated? And where? Then and then only can you go on to deal with what the document says'.

I have tried to follow these injunctions to the letter. It would be nice to think that Geoffrey's ghost might be reasonably pleased with the result and take it as a little peace offering.

PICTURE ACKNOWLEDGEMENTS

INDEX

An invitation from the publisher

Join us at www.hodder.co.uk, or follow us
on Twitter @hodderbooks to be a part of
our community of people who love the very
best in books and reading.

Whether you want to discover more about a book
or an author, watch trailers and interviews, have the
chance to win early limited editions, or simply browse
our expert readers' selection of the very best books,
we think you'll find what you're looking for.

And if you don't, that's the place to tell us what's missing.

We love what we do, and we'd love you to be a part of it.

www.hodder.co.uk

@hodderbooks

HodderBooks

HodderBooks